Christian
mission

IN THE MODERN WORLD

The substance of this book was given at the
World Congress on Evangelism at Lausanne
in 1974 and later at the Chevasse lectures in
Oxford in 1975. It examines the biblical
teaching on mission, evangelism, dialogue,
salvation and conversion and its practical
implications on organizations such as the
World Council of Churches.

JOHN R W STOTT

Christian mission

IN THE MODERN WORLD

⊞ FALCON

A FALCON BOOK

published by
Church Pastoral Aid Society
Falcon Court, 32 Fleet Street, London, EC4Y 1DB

distributed overseas by
Australia: Emu Book Agencies Ltd, 63 Berry Street, Granville,
NSW 2142
Canada: The Book Society of Canada, PO Box 200, Agincourt,
Ontario
New Zealand: Scripture Union Wholesale, PO Box 760,
Wellington
Singapore State: SU Christian Book Centre, 36H Prinsep Street,
Singapore
South Africa: SUBASA, 83 Camp Ground Road, Rondebosch
7700, Cape Town

Christian mission
IN THE MODERN WORLD

ISBN 0 85491 855 8
First published 1975
Second edition 1977
Text © J. R. W. Stott 1975

DESIGNED AND PRODUCED IN
THE UNITED KINGDOM
Filmset in 'Monophoto' Baskerville by
Richard Clay (The Chaucer Press), Ltd, Bungay, Suffolk
and printed by
Fletcher & Son Ltd, Norwich

Contents

Foreword

Each year, a distinguished visitor is invited to deliver at Wycliffe Hall, Oxford, a series of public lectures known as the Chavasse Lectures in World Mission. The 1975 Chavasse Lectures, were given by John Stott to a packed audience (and an overflow as well) drawn from the University of the city as well as from Wycliffe Hall itself. I am delighted that the Lectures are now being made available in book-form to a much wider public, and I am honoured by being invited to contribute a foreword.

John Stott's aim is to examine the biblical meaning of some of the great key words which are at the centre of the contemporary debate about Christian mission. In that debate, the interpretation of mission which is popular in some circles within the ecumenical movement differs acutely from that which has been held traditionally by many evangelicals. Sometimes the difference has seemed to amount to an impasse where further discussion is useless, and there is no hope of progress towards reconciliation. The way forward is for the two sides to meet together in joint study of the Scripture, and to correct and enrich their own and others' understanding of mission by a deeper understanding of the biblical missionary theme and a fuller submission to it. John Stott's lectures and now his book are a notable contribution to this enterprise.

As I listened to the lectures, four adjectives kept coming to me as I think they will to the readers of the book.

First, biblical. He goes direct to the Scriptures, works hard at the text and tries honestly not to read a meaning into it, but to read its own meaning out of it.

Secondly, clear. He is an exact and rigorous thinker who cuts through ambiguities and obscurities, and compels us to face theological issues, logically and precisely.

Thirdly, fair. He does not hesitate to criticize what is unbiblical in modern radical theology, but neither does he spare the unbiblical attitudes which sometimes lurk among the presuppositions and attitudes of evangelicals. He always qualifies his criticisms so as to avoid any injustice to those whom he criticizes and he balances criticism by generous recognition of the true and good things which those with whom he disagrees are saying and standing for.

Fourthly, constructive. He speaks and writes with the courtesy and warm friendship which Christians owe to one another when they are discussing their differences. He is not concerned to defend his own position, nor to defeat someone else's. Rather, he is inviting us to learn together more of God's truth and together we open ourselves more fully to the biblical revelation of Jesus Christ. It is in this way that ecumenical discussions can be positive and fruitful, and can help the church to be renewed in unity for mission. It is good to have this contribution to ecumenical understanding from an Evangelical source, and I hope that the book will be widely read both by evangelicals and radicals for we can all learn a great deal from it.

J. P. Hickinbotham
Principal, Wycliffe Hall, Oxford

Preface

Apart from my personal commitment to evangelism, both to evangelism through the local church and—since a mission in Cambridge University in 1952—to university evangelism, there are four particular experiences which have contributed to the writing of this book.

First, in 1968 I attended as an 'adviser' the Fourth Assembly of the World Council of Churches at Uppsala. Finding myself allocated to Section II ('Renewal in Mission'), I was immediately plunged into the thick of contemporary debate about the meaning of mission.

Then, although I was not able to attend the 'Salvation Today' conference at Bangkok in January 1973, I naturally followed it with deep interest and concern. When invited the following year to deliver the annual Baker lecture in Melbourne (in memory of Bishop Donald Baker, New Testament scholar and former Principal of Ridley College, Melbourne), I chose as my theme 'Salvation Yesterday and Today'. The substance of this lecture is reproduced with permission, and enlarged, in Chapter 4.

Thirdly, the Planning Committee of the International Congress on World Evangelisation at Lausanne in July 1974 asked me to give an opening address on 'the nature of biblical evangelism,' and to seek to provide a biblical definition of the five words 'mission,' 'evangelism,' 'dialogue,' 'salvation' and 'conversion.'

So when, fourthly, Canon Jim Hickinbotham, Principal of Wycliffe Hall, Oxford, invited me to deliver the 1975 Chavasse Lectures (in memory both of Bishop F. J. Chavasse of Liverpool who had been Principal of Wycliffe Hall and of his son Bishop Christopher Chavasse who had been Master of St Peter's College and Chairman of the governing body of Wycliffe Hall), it seemed appropriate to take the same five words and elaborate what I had attempted to sketch at Lausanne. I am very grateful to the Principal, staff and students of Wycliffe Hall for the kindly welcome and attentive hearing which they gave me, and for the stimulus of the question-time which followed each lecture. I am also very grateful to Jim Hickinbotham for the generous terms in which he has written his foreword.

Although I have no wish to disguise myself or to conceal that I am a Christian of 'evangelical' conviction, this book is not an exercise in party propaganda. I have no axe to grind, except to go on seeking to discover what the Spirit is saying through the Word to the churches. Nothing encouraged me more at Wycliffe than to hear the Principal's concluding comment that he thought I had been 'scrupulously fair' towards those with whom I have ventured to disagree. This has certainly been my aim. Besides, if I am critical of others, I desire also to be critical of myself and of my fellow evangelicals. Life is a pilgrimage of learning, a voyage of discovery, in which our mistaken views are corrected, our distorted notions adjusted, our shallow opinions deepened and some of our vast ignorances diminished.

Perhaps the greatest need in current ecumenical debate is to find an agreed biblical hermeneutic, for without this a broader consensus on the meaning and obligation of 'mission' is unlikely ever to be reached.

J.R.W.S.

April 1975

Introduction: words and their meanings

All Christians everywhere, whatever their cultural background or theological persuasion, must think at some time or other about the relation between the church and the world. Whether our particular context is the post-Christian secularism of the so-called free world, or some form of Marxism in the Communist bloc, or a culture permeated by Hinduism, Buddhism or Islam in one of the nations of the Third World, the same unavoidable questions trouble the Christian conscience: what should be the church's relation to the world? What is a Christian's responsibility towards his non-Christian relatives, friends and neighbours, and indeed to the whole non-Christian community?

In reply to these questions most Christians would make some use of the term 'mission.' One can hardly discuss church–world relations and omit the concept of 'mission.' But there would be a wide divergence in our understanding of what our 'mission' is, of what part 'evangelism' plays in mission, and of what part 'dialogue' plays in evangelism. I fear further that we would diverge from one another not only in our understanding of the *nature* of mission, evangelism and dialogue, but also in our understanding of the *goal* of all three. Possibly the terms 'conversion' and 'salvation' would figure somewhere in our definition of goals, but again there might be little consensus regarding the meaning of these words. My task then, is to take this cluster of five words—mission, evangelism, dialogue, salvation and conversion—and to attempt to define them biblically. As I said at Lausanne, I am anxious that my purpose should not be misunderstood. We are all aware that during the last few years especially since the Fourth Assembly of the World Council of Churches at Uppsala in 1968, relations between ecumen-

ical and evangelical Christians (if I may use these terms as
a convenient shorthand, for I recognize that they are by
no means mutually exclusive) have hardened into something like a confrontation. I have no wish to worsen this
situation. Nor, I hope, shall I resort to the dubious device
of putting up a few ecumenical skittles in order to knock
them down with well-aimed evangelical balls, so that we
can all applaud our easy victory! Mind you, I believe that
some current ecumenical thinking is mistaken. But then,
candidly, I believe some of our traditional evangelical
formulations are mistaken also. Many ecumenical
Christians do not seem to have begun to learn to live
under the authority of Scripture. We evangelicals think
we have—and there is no doubt we sincerely want to—-
but at some times we are very selective in our submission,
and at others the traditions of the evangelical elders seem
to owe more to culture than to Scripture. My chief concern, therefore, is to bring both ecumenical and evangelical thinking to the same independent and objective
test, namely that of the biblical revelation.

My starting-point, however, is not the word of God but
the wisdom of Alice—of Alice in Wonderland, that is, or
more precisely of Alice Through the Looking Glass. You
may recall her spirited exchange with Humpty Dumpty:

'When *I* use a word,' Humpty Dumpty said in a rather scornful
tone, 'it means just what I choose it to mean, neither more nor
less.'
'The question is,' said Alice, 'whether you *can* make words mean
different things.'
'The question is,' said Humpty Dumpty, 'which is to be master—that's all.'

It is instructive to ponder this conversation. Alice and
Humpty Dumpty began by discussing the word 'glory'
(which Humpty Dumpty told Alice with a contemptuous
smile she of course did not understand until he told her
what it meant), then the word 'impenetrability' (which
Humpty Dumpty pressed into meaning so many things
that he added 'When I make a word do a lot of work like
that, I always pay it extra'), and finally the poem
'Jabberwocky' (which prompted Humpty Dumpty to say

that some words are 'like a portmanteau—there are two meanings packed up into one word').

Americans might well dub Humpty Dumpty a 'sophomore,' for he was a strange mixture of wisdom and folly, sense and nonsense. He was entirely right that some words *are* like portmanteaux, and that others deserve extra pay because of the amount of work they have to do. But he was entirely wrong to imagine that he was the master of words and could impose meanings on them arbitrarily, according to his own whimsical choice.

Yet (dare I say it?) some modern theologians appear to be as perverse as Humpty Dumpty in their use of biblical words. If I had a fraction of Lewis Carroll's imagination, I think I might attempt a parody entitled 'Malice in Wonderland' or 'Adventures into theological fantasy.'

It is not disputed that time changes the meaning of words. 'The ideal of "timeless English," ' wrote C. S. Lewis in one of his *Letters to Malcolm* (Collins) 'is sheer nonsense. No living language can be timeless. You might as well ask for a motionless river.'

No modern writer has demonstrated this more forcefully than Alvin Toffler in his *Future Shock* (Bodley Head, 1970). He has a fascinating section on the transience of human language called 'The semi-literate Shakespeare' in which he quotes Stuart Berg Flexner, the senior editor of the Random House Dictionary of the English Language: 'were Shakespeare suddenly to materialize in London or New York today, he would be able to understand on the average only 5 out of every 9 words in our vocabulary. The Bard would be a semi-literate.'

What Messrs Lewis, Flexner and Toffler are saying is that the meaning of words evolves. What a word means today is probably very different from what it meant yesterday, still more the day before yesterday and the day before that. But the recognition that today's meaning is different from yesterday's gives us no warrant to confuse the two, or to read today's meaning back into yesterday's word. On the contrary, yesterday's word has yesterday's meaning, and today's word today's meaning.

When this elementary principle is applied to biblical interpretation, it is usually graced with the rather grandiose expression 'grammatico-historical exegesis.' Negatively, this indicates that we have no liberty to impose on biblical words meanings they were never intended to bear. Positively, it lays upon us the discipline of studying words in both their grammatical context and their historical setting. It is grammar and history together which determine the meaning of words, as every lawyer trained in the interpretation of documents will confirm. E. D. Hirsch sums it up in his book *Validity in Interpretation* (Yale University Press, 1967): 'a text means what its author meant.'

1 Mission

The first word we have to consider is 'mission.' Before attempting a biblical definition it may be helpful to take a look at the contemporary polarization.

TWO EXTREME VIEWS

The older or traditional view has been to equate mission and evangelism, missionaries and evangelists, missions and evangelistic programmes. Even the Commission on World Mission and Evangelism did not distinguish in its constitution between 'mission' and 'evangelism,' but defined its aim as 'to further the proclamation to the whole world of the gospel of Jesus Christ, to the end that all men may believe in him and be saved.' As Philip Potter said in his address to the wcc Central Committee, meeting in Crete in 1967, 'ecumenical literature since Amsterdam has used "mission," "witness" and "evangelism" interchangeably.'

In its extreme form this older view of mission as consisting exclusively of evangelism also concentrated on verbal proclamation. The missionary was often caricatured as standing under a palm tree, wearing a sola topi, and declaiming the gospel to a group of ill-clad natives sitting respectfully round him on the ground. Thus the traditional image of the missionary was of the preacher, and a rather paternalistic kind of preacher at that. Such an emphasis on the priority of evangelistic preaching left little room in some cases even for the founding of Christian schools. Philip Crowe told us at the 1968 Islington Conference of a certain R. N. Cust who argued in 1888 that missionary money 'was collected for the purpose of converting a soul, not sharpening an intellect.' He slightly modified his position in 1894 to include 'a lay evangelist, a female evangelist, a medical evangelist whenever gospel preaching is the substantive work,' but added: 'when it is proposed to have a pious industrial superintendent, or an evangelical tile manufacturer, or a low church breeder of cattle or raiser of turnips, I draw my line' (*Mission in the Modern World*, Patmos, 1968).

This is a very extreme example, however. Most adherents of the traditional view of mission would regard education and medical work as perfectly proper, and indeed as very useful adjuncts to evangelistic work, often out of Christian compassion for the ignorant and the sick, though sometimes as being unashamedly 'platforms' or 'springboards' for evangelism—hospitals and schools providing in their patients and pupils a conveniently captive audience for the gospel. In either case the mission itself was understood in terms of evangelism.

This traditional view is far from being dead and buried. The so-called 'Jesus movement' has encouraged the formation of Christian communes into which zealous young evangelicals withdraw from the wicked world. For a commune easily degenerates into a compound, and even into a quasi-monastic establishment. Then the only contact which such Christians have with the world (which they regard as totally and irredeemably wicked) is to make occasional evangelistic raids into it. Apocalyptic imagery comes natural to them. The world is like a building on fire, they say; a Christian's only duty is to mount a rescue operation before it is too late. Jesus Christ is coming at any moment; there is no point in tampering with the structures of society, for society is doomed and about to be destroyed. Besides, any attempt to improve society is bound to be unproductive since unrenewed men cannot build a new world. Man's only hope lies in being born again. Only then might society conceivably be reborn. But it is too late now even for that.

Such world-denying pessimism is a strange phenomenon in those who say they believe in God. But then their image of God is only partially shaped by the biblical revelation. He is not the Creator who in the beginning gave man a 'cultural mandate' to subdue and rule the earth, who has instituted governing authorities as his 'ministers' to order society and maintain justice, and who, as the Lausanne Covenant puts it, because he is 'both the Creator and the Judge of all men' is concerned for 'justice and reconciliation throughout human society' (para. 5).

At the opposite extreme to this unbiblical concept of mission as consisting of evangelism alone there is the standard ecumenical viewpoint, at least since the middle 1960s and the preparatory work for the Uppsala Assembly. The publication in 1967 of the reports of the West European and North American working groups on 'the missionary structure of the congregation,' entitled *The Church for Others* (WCC), gave currency to a whole new vocabulary of mission. The thesis developed in these reports was that God is at work in the historical process, that the purpose of his mission, of the *missio Dei*, is the establishment of *shalom* (Hebrew for 'peace') in the sense of social harmony, and that this *shalom* (which it was suggested is identical with the kingdom of God) is exemplified in 'the emancipation of coloured races, the concern for the humanization of industrial relations, various attempts at rural development, the quest for business and professional ethics, the concern for intellectual honesty and integrity.'

Moreover, in working towards this goal God uses 'men and women both inside and outside the churches,' and the church's particular role in the mission of God is to 'point to God at work in world history,' to discover what he is doing, to catch up with it and to get involved in it ourselves. For God's primary relationship is to the world, it was argued, so that the true sequence is to be found no longer in the formula 'God–church–world' but in the formula 'God–world–church.' This being so, 'it is the world that must be allowed to provide the agenda for the churches'—the churches taking the world seriously and seeking to serve according to its contemporary sociological needs.

Professor J. G. Davies, who had been a member of the West European working group, expressed similar ideas in his two books *Worship and Mission* (SCM, 1966) and *Dialogue with the World* (SCM, 1967). He equated humanization, reconciliation, *shalom* and the setting up of God's kingdom as being together the goal of mission (*Dialogue*). 'Hence mission is concerned with the overcoming of industrial disputes, with the surmounting of class divisions, with the eradication of racial discrimination.' Indeed, 'we are required to enter into partnership with God in history to renew society.'

Much of this attempted reconstruction of 'mission' was quoted in the *Drafts for Sections*, which were published in preparation for Uppsala. Mission was seen as the historical process of the renewal of society, and the theme text of Uppsala was 'Behold, I make all things new' (Revelation 21:5). But this word of God is an eschatological affirmation. It is uttered from the throne (in John's vision), almost immediately after the new heaven and the new earth have appeared. Yet several times at Uppsala it was used as an expression not of future hope but of present reality, not of the final regeneration of the universe but of 'the acceleration of social and political change.'

Apart from this misuse of Scripture, what are we to say about the identification of the mission of God with social renewal? A fourfold critique may be made. First, the God who is the Lord of history is also the Judge of history. It is naïve to hail all revolutionary movements as signs of divine renewal. After the revolution the new status quo sometimes enshrines more injustice and oppression than the one it has displaced.

Secondly, the biblical categories of *shalom*, the new humanity and the kingdom of God are not to be identified with social renewal. It is true that in the Old Testament *shalom* (peace) often indicates political and material well-being. But can it be maintained, as serious biblical exegesis, that the New Testament authors present Jesus Christ as winning this kind of peace and as bestowing it on society as a whole? To assume that all Old Testament prophecies are fulfilled in literal and material terms is to make the very mistake which Jesus's contemporaries made when they tried to take him by force and make him a king (John 6:15). The New Testament understanding of Old Testament prophecy is that its fulfilment *transcends* the categories in which the promises were given. So according to the apostles the peace which Jesus preaches and gives is something deeper and richer, namely reconciliation and fellowship with God and with each other (*eg* Ephesians 2:13–22). Moreover, he does not bestow it on all men but on those who belong to him, to his redeemed community. So *shalom* is the blessing the Messiah brings to his people. The new creation and the new humanity are to be seen in those who are in Christ (2 Corinthians 5:17); and the kingdom has to be received like a little child (Mark 10:15). Certainly it is our Christian duty to commend by argument and example the righteous standards of the kingdom to those who have not themselves received or entered it. In this way we see the righteousness of the kingdom, as it were, 'spilling over' into segments of the world and thus to some extent blurring the frontiers be-tween the two. Nevertheless the kingdom remains distinct from godless society, and actual entry into it depends on spiritual rebirth.

Thirdly, the word 'mission' cannot properly be used to cover everything God is doing in the world. In providence and common grace he is indeed active in all men and all societies, whether they acknowledge him or not. But this is not his 'mission.' 'Mission' concerns his redeemed people, and what he sends *them* into the world to do.

Fourthly, Uppsala's preoccupation with social change left little or no room for evangelistic concern. It was this imbalance against which, if I may speak personally, I felt I had to protest at the plenary session at which the report of Section II 'Renewal in Mission' was made.

The Assembly has given its earnest attention to the hunger, poverty and injustices of the contemporary world [*I said*]. Rightly so. I have myself been moved by it. But I do not find a comparable concern or compassion for the spiritual hunger of men . . . The church's first priority . . . remains the millions and millions . . . who (as Christ and his apostles tell us again and again) being without Christ are perishing . . . The World Council of Churches professes to acknowledge Jesus Christ as Lord. Well, the Lord Jesus Christ sent his church to preach the good news and make disciples; I do not see this Assembly as a whole eager to obey his command. The Lord Jesus Christ wept over the impenitent city which had rejected him; I do not see this Assembly weeping any similar tears.

A BIBLICAL SYNTHESIS?

From the traditional view of mission as exclusively evangelistic and the current ecumenical view of it as the establishment of *shalom*, we ask if there is a better way, a more balanced and more biblical way of defining the mission of the church, and of relating to one another the evangelistic and social responsibilities of the people of God. The delegates to the meeting of the Commission on World Mission and Evangelism in Mexico City in December 1963 saw the problem, but said they were unable to find a solution. They confessed in the report of Section III:

Debate returned again and again to the relationship between God's action in and through the Church and everything God is doing in the world apparently independently of the Christian community. Can a distinction be drawn between God's providential action and God's redeeming action? . . . We were able to state thesis and antithesis in this debate, but we could not see our way through to the truth which we feel lies beyond this dialectic.
'Witness in Six Continents' edited by
R. K. Orchard, Edinburgh House Press, 1964

Many came to Uppsala hoping for a genuine meeting of minds by which this tension could be resolved. In one of the opening speeches Dr W. A. Visser t'Hooft expressed the hope that the Assembly would deal with this issue 'positively and ecumenically'—'positively in the sense that we give a clear sense of orientation to our movement' and 'ecumenically in the sense that we will truly listen to each other.' He went on to make his own contribution by saying:

I believe that, with regard to the great tension between the vertical interpretation of the Gospel as essentially concerned with God's saving action in the life of individuals, and the horizontal interpretation of it as mainly concerned with human relationships in the world, we must get out of that rather primitive oscillating movement of going from one extreme to the other, which is not worthy of a movement which by its nature seeks to embrace the truth of the gospel in its fulness. A Christianity which has lost its vertical dimension has lost its salt and is not only insipid in itself, but useless for the world. But a Christianity which would use the vertical preoccupation as a means to escape from its responsibility for and in the common

life of man is a denial of the incarnation, of God's love for the
world manifested in Christ.

'The Uppsala 68 Report' edited by Norman Goodall, WCC, *1968*

But unfortunately what Mexico left unfinished Uppsala
did not complete, and Dr Visser t'Hooft's hope was
unfulfilled. The old polarization continues.

All of us should be able to agree that mission arises
primarily out of the nature not of the church but of God
himself. The living God of the Bible is a sending God. I
think it was Johannes Blauw in his book *The Missionary
Nature of the Church* (McGraw-Hill, 1962) who first used
the word 'centrifugal' to describe the church's mission.
Then Professor J. G. Davies applied it to God himself.
God, he writes, is 'a centrifugal Being' (*Worship and
Mission,* 1966). It is a dramatic figure of speech. Yet it is
only another way of saying that God is love, always reach-
ing out after others in self-giving service.

So he sent forth Abraham, commanding him to go from
his country and kindred into the great unknown, and
promising to bless him and to bless the world through him
if he obeyed (Genesis 12:1-3). Next, he sent Joseph into
Egypt, overruling even his brothers' cruelty, in order to
preserve a godly remnant on earth during the famine
(Genesis 45:4-8). Then he sent Moses to his oppressed
people in Egypt, with good news of liberation, saying to
him: 'Come, I will send you to Pharaoh that you may
bring forth my people . . . out of Egypt' (Exodus 3:10).
After the Exodus and the settlement he sent a continuous
succession of prophets with words of warning and of
promise to his people. As he said through Jeremiah: 'From
the day that your fathers came out of the land of Egypt to
this day, I have persistently sent all my servants the prophets to them, day after day, yet they did not listen to
me . . .' (Jeremiah 7:25, 26 *cf* 2 Chronicles 36:15, 16).
After the Babylonian captivity he graciously sent them
back to the land, and sent more messengers with them
and to them to help them rebuild the temple, the city and
the national life. Then at last 'when the time had fully
come, God sent forth his Son'; and after that the Father
and the Son sent forth the Spirit on the Day of Pentecost
(Galatians 4:4-6; John 14:26; 15:26; 16:7; Acts 2:33).

All this is the essential biblical background to any understanding of mission. The primal mission is God's, for it is he who sent his prophets, his Son, his Spirit. Of these missions the mission of the Son is central, for it was the culmination of the ministry of the prophets, and it embraced within itself as its climax the sending of the Spirit. And now the Son sends as he himself was sent. Already during his public ministry he sent out first the apostles and then the seventy as a kind of extension of his own preaching, teaching and healing ministry. Then after his death and resurrection he widened the scope of the mission to include all who call him Lord and themselves his disciples. For others were present with the twelve when the Great Commission was given (*eg* Luke 24:33). We cannot restrict its application to the apostles.

THE GREAT COMMISSION
This brings us to a consideration of the terms of the Great Commission. What was it that the Lord Jesus commissioned his people to do? There can be no doubt that most versions of it (for he seems to have repeated it in several forms on several occasions) place the emphasis on evangelism. 'Go into all the world and preach the gospel to the whole creation' is the familiar command of the 'longer ending' of Mark's gospel which seems to have been added by some later hand after Mark's original conclusion was lost (Mark 16:15). 'Go . . . and make disciples of all nations, baptizing them . . . and teaching them . . .' is the Matthean form (Matthew 28:19, 20), while Luke records at the end of his gospel Christ's word 'that repentance and forgiveness of sins should be preached in his name to all nations' and at the beginning of the Acts that his people would receive power to become his witnesses to the end of the earth (Luke 24:47; Acts 1:8). The cumulative emphasis seems clear. It is placed on preaching, witnessing and making disciples, and many deduce from this that the mission of the church, according to the specification of the risen Lord, is exclusively a preaching, converting and teaching mission. Indeed, I confess that I myself argued this at the World Congress on Evangelism in Berlin in

1966, when attempting to expound the three major versions of the Great Commission.

Today, however, I would express myself differently. It is not just that the commission includes a duty to teach converts everything Jesus had previously commanded (Matthew 28:20), and that social reponsibility is among the things which Jesus commanded. I now see more clearly that not only the consequences of the commission but the actual commission itself must be understood to include social as well as evangelistic responsibility, unless we are to be guilty of distorting the words of Jesus.

The crucial form in which the Great Commission has been handed down to us (though it is the most neglected because it is the most costly) is the Johannine. Jesus had anticipated it in his prayer in the upper room when he said to the Father: 'As thou didst send me into the world, so I have sent them into the world' (John 17:18). Now, probably in the same upper room but after his death and resurrection, he turned his prayer-statement into a commission and said: 'As the Father has sent me, even so I send you' (John 20:21). In both these sentences Jesus did more than draw a vague parallel between his mission and ours. Deliberately and precisely he made his mission the *model* of ours, saying '*as* the Father sent me, *so* I send you.' Therefore our understanding of the church's mission must be deduced from our understanding of the Son's. Why and how did the Father send the Son?

Of course the major purpose of the Son's coming into the world was unique. Perhaps it is partly for this reason that Christians have been hesitant to think of their mission as in any sense comparable to his. For the Father sent the Son to be the Saviour of the world, and to that end to atone for our sins and to bring us eternal life (1 John 4:9, 10, 14). Indeed, he himself said he had come 'to seek and to save the lost' (Luke 19:10). We cannot copy him in these things. We are not saviours. Nevertheless, all this is still an inadequate statement of why he came.

It is better to begin with something more general and say that he came to serve. His contemporaries were familiar with Daniel's apocalyptic vision of the son of man

receiving dominion and being served by all peoples
(Daniel 7:14). But Jesus knew he had to serve before he
would be served, and to endure suffering before he would
receive dominion. So he fused two apparently incompatible Old Testament images, Daniel's son of man and
Isaiah's suffering servant, and said: 'the Son of man . . .
came not to be served but to serve, and to give his life a
ransom for many' (Mark 10:45). The ransoming sin-
offering was a sacrifice which he alone could offer, but this
was to be the climax of a life of service, and we too may
serve. 'I am among you' he said on another occasion 'as
one who serves' (Luke 22:27). So he gave himself in
selfless service for others, and his service took a wide variety of forms according to men's needs. Certainly he
preached, proclaiming the good news of the kingdom of
God and teaching about the coming and the nature of the
kingdom, how to enter it and how it would spread. But he
served in deed as well as in word, and it would be impossible in the ministry of Jesus to separate his works from his
words. He fed hungry mouths and washed dirty feet, he
healed the sick, comforted the sad and even restored the
dead to life.

Now he sends us, he says, as the Father had sent him.
Therefore our mission, like his, is to be one of service. He
emptied himself of status and took the form of a servant,
and his humble mind is to be in us (Philippians 2:5–8). He
supplies us with the perfect model of service, and sends his
church into the world to be a servant church. Is it not
essential for us to recover this biblical emphasis? In many
of our Christian attitudes and enterprises we have tended
(especially those of us who live in Europe and North
America) to be rather bosses than servants. Yet it seems
that it is in our servant role that we can find the right
synthesis of evangelism and social action. For both should
be for us, as they undoubtedly were for Christ, authentic
expressions of the love that serves.

Then there is another aspect of the mission of the Son
which is to be paralleled in the mission of the church,
namely that in order to serve he was sent *into the world*. He
did not touch down like a visitor from outer space, or
arrive like an alien, bringing his own alien culture with

him. He took to himself our humanity, our flesh and blood, our culture. He actually became one of us and experienced our frailty, our suffering and our temptations. He even bore our sin and died our death. And now he sends us 'into the world,' to identify with others as he identified with us (though without losing our Christian identity), to become vulnerable as he did. It is surely one of the most characteristic failures of us Christians, not least of us who are called evangelical Christians, that we seldom seem to take seriously this principle of the Incarnation. 'As our Lord took on our flesh,' runs the report from Mexico City 1963, 'so he calls his Church to take on the secular world. This is easy to say and sacrificial to do' (*Witness in Six Continents*). It comes more natural to us to shout the gospel at people from a distance than to involve ourselves deeply in their lives, to think ourselves into their culture and their problems, and to feel with them in their pains. Yet this implication of our Lord's example is inescapable. As the Lausanne Covenant put it: 'We affirm that Christ sends his redeemed people into the world as the Father sent him, and that this calls for a similar deep and costly penetration of the world' (para. 6).

THE RELATION BETWEEN EVANGELISM AND SOCIAL ACTION

What, then, should be the relation between evangelism and social action within our total Christian responsibility? If we grant that we have no liberty either to concentrate on evangelism to the exclusion of social concern or to make social activism a substitute for evangelism, we still need to define the relation between the two. Three main ways of doing this have been attempted.

First, some regard social action as *a means to evangelism*. In this case evangelism and the winning of converts are the primary ends in view, but social action is a useful preliminary, an effective means to these ends. In its most blatant form this makes social work (whether food, medicine or education) the sugar on the pill, the bait on the hook, while in its best form it gives to the gospel a credibility it would otherwise lack. In either case the smell of hypocrisy hangs round our philanthropy. A frankly ulterior motive impels us to engage in it. And the result of making our social programme the means to another end is that we breed so-called 'rice Christians.' This is inevitable if we ourselves have been 'rice evangelists.' They caught the deception from us. No wonder Gandhi said in 1931: 'I hold that proselytizing under the cloak of humanitarian work is, to say the least, unhealthy . . . why should I change my religion because a doctor who professes Christianity as his religion has cured me of some disease . . .?'

The second way of relating evangelism and social action is better. It regards social action not as a means to evangelism but as *a manifestation of evangelism*, or at least of the gospel which is being proclaimed. In this case philanthropy is not attached to evangelism rather artificially from the outside, but grows out of it as its natural expression. One might almost say that social action becomes the 'sacrament' of evangelism, for it makes the message significantly visible. J. Herman Bavinck in his famous book *An Introduction to the Science of Missions* (published 1954 in Holland, and 1960 by the Presbyterian and Reformed Publishing Co.) defends this view. Medicine and education are more than 'a legitimate and necessary means of creating an opportunity for preaching,' he writes, for 'if these services are motivated by the proper love and compassion, then they cease to be simply preparation, and at that very moment become preaching.' We should not hesitate to agree with this, so far as it goes, for there is a strong precedent for it in the ministry of Jesus. His words and deeds belonged to each other, the words interpreting the deeds and the deeds embodying the words. He did not only announce the good news of the kingdom; he performed visible 'signs of the kingdom.' If people would not believe his words, he said, then let them believe him 'for the sake of the works themselves' (John 14:11).

Bishop John V. Taylor takes a somewhat similar line in his contribution to the 'Christian Foundations' series entitled *For All the World* (Hodder and Stoughton, 1966).

He writes of a 'three-stranded presentation of the Gospel,' by which he means that Christians are called to 'articulate the gospel . . . through what they say (proclamation), what they are (witness) and what they do (service).' This also is true, and finely said. Yet it leaves me uneasy. For it makes service a subdivision of evangelism, an aspect of the proclamation. I do not deny that good works of love did have an evidential value when performed by Jesus and do have an evidential value when performed by us (*cf* Matthew 5:16). But I cannot bring myself to accept that this is their only or even major justification. If it is, then still, and rather self-consciously at that, they are only a means to an end. If good works are visible preaching, then they are expecting a return; but if good works are visible loving, then they are 'expecting nothing in return' (Luke 6:35).

This brings me to the third way of stating the relation between evangelism and social action, which I believe to be the truly Christian one, namely that social action is *a partner of evangelism*. As partners the two belong to each other and yet are independent of each other. Each stands on its own feet in its own right alongside the other. Neither is a means to the other, or even a manifestation of the other. For each is an end in itself. Both are expressions of unfeigned love. As the National Evangelical Anglican Congress at Keele put it in 1967: 'Evangelism and compassionate service belong together in the mission of God' (para. 2.20).

The apostle John has helped me to grasp this by these words from his first letter: 'If any one has the world's goods and sees his brother in need, yet closes his heart against him, how does God's love abide in him? Little children, let us not love in word or speech but in deed and in truth' (1 John 3:17, 18). Here love in action springs from a twofold situation, first 'seeing' a brother in need and secondly 'having' the wherewithal to meet the need. If I do not relate what I 'have' to what I 'see,' I cannot claim to be indwelt by the love of God. Further, this principle applies whatever the nature of the seen need. I may see spiritual need (sin, guilt, lostness) and have the gospel knowledge to meet it. Or the need I see may be disease or ignorance or bad housing, and I may have the medical, educational or social expertise to relieve it. To see need and to possess the remedy compels love to act, and whether the action will be evangelistic or social, or indeed political, depends on what we 'see' and what we 'have.'

This does not mean that words and works, evangelism and social action, are such inseparable partners that all of us must engage in both all the time. Situations vary, and so do Christian callings. As for situations, there will be times when a person's eternal destiny is the most urgent consideration, for we must not forget that men without Christ are perishing. But there will certainly be other times when a person's material need is so pressing that he would not be able to hear the gospel if we shared it with him. The man who fell among robbers needed above all else at that moment oil and bandages for his wounds, not evangelistic tracts in his pockets! Similarly, in the words of a missionary in Nairobi quoted by Bishop John Taylor, 'a hungry man has no ears.' If our enemy is hungry, our biblical mandate is not to evangelize him but to feed him (Romans 12:20)! Then too there is a diversity of Christian callings, and every Christian should be faithful to his own calling. The doctor must not neglect the practice of medicine for evangelism, not should the evangelist be distracted from the ministry of the word by the ministry of tables, as the apostles quickly discovered (Acts 6).

THE GREAT COMMANDMENT

Let me return now to the Great Commission. I have tried to argue that its Johannine form, according to which the church's mission is to be modelled on the Son's, implies that we are sent into the world to serve, and that the humble service we are to render will include for us as it did for Christ both words and works, a concern for the hunger and for the sickness of both body and soul, in other words, both evangelistic and social activity. But supposing someone remains convinced that the Great Commission relates exclusively to evangelism, what then?

I venture to say that sometimes, perhaps because it was the last instruction Jesus gave us before returning to the

Father, we give the Great Commission too prominent a place in our Christian thinking. Please do not misunderstand me. I firmly believe that the whole church is under obligation to obey its Lord's commission to take the gospel to all nations. But I am also concerned that we should not regard this as the only instruction which Jesus left us. He also quoted Leviticus 19:18 'you shall love your neighbour as yourself,' called it 'the second and great commandment' (second in importance only to the supreme command to love God with all our being), and elaborated it in the Sermon on the Mount. There he insisted that in God's vocabulary our neighbour includes our enemy, and that to love means to 'do good,' that is, to give ourselves actively and constructively to serve our neighbour's welfare.

Here then are two instructions of Jesus—a great commandment 'love your neighbour' and a great commission 'go and make disciples.' What is the relation between the two? Some of us behave as if we thought them identical, so that if we share the gospel with somebody, we consider we have completed our responsibility to love him. But no. The Great Commission neither explains, nor exhausts, nor supersedes the Great Commandment. What it does is to add to the requirement of neighbour-love and neighbour-service a new and urgent Christian dimension. If we truly love our neighbour we shall without doubt share with him the good news of Jesus. How can we possibly claim to love him if we know the gospel but keep it from him? Equally, however, if we truly love our neighbour we shall not stop with evangelism. Our neighbour is neither a bodyless soul that we should love only his soul, nor a soulless body that we should care for its welfare alone, nor even a body-soul isolated from society. God created man, who is my neighbour, a body-soul-in-community. Therefore, if we love our neighbour as God made him, we must inevitably be concerned for his total welfare, the good of his soul, his body and his community. Moreover, it is this vision of man as a social being, as well as a psycho-somatic being, which obliges us to add a *political* dimension to our social concern. Humanitarian activity cares for the casualties of a sick society. We should be concerned with preventive medicine or community health as well, which means the quest for better social structures in which peace, dignity, freedom and justice are secured for all men. And there is no reason why, in pursuing this quest, we should not join hands with all men of good will, even if they are not Christians.

To sum up, we are sent into the world, like Jesus, to serve. For this is the natural expression of our love for our neighbours. We love. We go. We serve. And in this we have (or should have) no ulterior motive. True, the gospel lacks visibility if we merely preach it, and lacks credibility if we who preach it are interested only in souls and have no concern about the welfare of people's bodies, situations and communities. Yet the reason for our acceptance of social responsibility is not primarily in order to give the gospel either a visibility or a credibility it would otherwise lack, but rather simple uncomplicated compassion. Love has no need to justify itself. It merely expresses itself in service wherever it sees need.

'Mission,' then, is not a word for everything the church does. 'The church is mission' sounds fine, but it's an over-statement. For the church is a worshipping as well as a serving community, and although worship and service belong together they are not to be confused. Nor, as we have seen, does 'mission' cover everything God does in the world. For God the Creator is constantly active in his world in providence, in common grace and in judgment, quite apart from the purposes for which he has sent his Son, his Spirit and his church into the world. 'Mission' describes rather everything the church is sent into the world to do. 'Mission' embraces the church's double voca-tion of service to be 'the salt of the earth' and 'the light of the world.' For Christ *sends* his people into the earth to be its salt, and *sends* his people into the world to be its light (Matthew 5:13–16).

PRACTICAL IMPLICATIONS

In conclusion, it may be helpful to consider what the realistic outworkings of this understanding of 'mission' are likely to be. Evangelical Christians are now repenting of the former pietism which tended to keep us insulated from the secular world, and are accepting that we have a social as well as an evangelistic responsibility. But what will this mean in practice? I would like to explore three areas— vocational, local and national.

I begin with vocation, by which I mean a Christian's life-work. We are often given the impression that if a young Christian man is really keen for Christ he will un- doubtedly become a foreign missionary, that if he is not quite as keen as that he will stay at home and become a pastor, that if he lacks the dedication to be a pastor, he will no doubt serve as a doctor or a teacher, while those who end up in social work or the media or (worst of all) in politics are not far removed from serious backsliding! It seems to me urgent to gain a truer perspective in this matter of vocation. Jesus Christ calls all his disciples to 'ministry,' that is, to service. He himself is the Servant par excellence, and he calls us to be servants too. This much then is certain: if we are Christians, we must spend our lives in the service of God and man. The only difference between us lies in the nature of the service we are called to render. Some are indeed called to be missionaries, evan- gelists or pastors, and others to the great professions of law, education, medicine and the social sciences. But others are called to commerce, to industry and farming, to accountancy and banking, to local government or par- liament, and to the mass media, while there are still many girls who find their vocation in homemaking and parent- hood without pursuing an independent career as well. In all these spheres, and many others besides, it is possible for Christians to interpret their lifework christianly, and to see it neither as a necessary evil (necessary, that is, for survival), nor even as a useful place in which to evangelize or make money for evangelism, but as their Christian vocation, as the way Christ has called them to spend their lives in his service. Further, a part of their calling will be to seek to maintain Christ's standards of justice, righ- teousness, honesty, human dignity and compassion in a society which no longer accepts them.

When any community deteriorates, the blame should be attached where it belongs: not to the community which is going bad but to the church which is failing in its responsibility as salt to stop it going bad. And the salt will be effective only if it permeates society, only if Christians learn again the wide diversity of divine callings, and if many penetrate deeply into secular society in order to serve Christ there.

To this end I would personally like to see the appointment of Christian vocation officers who would visit schools, colleges and churches not to recruit for the pastorate only but to set before young people the exciting variety of opportunities available today for serving Christ and their fellow human beings. I would also like to see regular vocation conferences, not *missionary* conferences only which accord the top priority to becoming a cross-cultural missionary, nor *ministry* conferences which concentrate on the ordained pastorate, but *mission* conferences which portray the biblical breadth of the mission of God, apply it to today's world, and challenge young people to give their lives unreservedly to service in some aspect of the Christian mission.

A second application concerns the local church. Here again our tendency has been to see the church as a worshipping and witnessing community, its responsibility to the parish or district being largely restricted to evangelistic witness. But if the local church is 'sent' into its area as the Father sent the Son into the world, its mission of service is wider than evangelism. Once the local church as a whole recognizes and accepts this fuller dimension of its responsibility, it is ready for a further truth. Although all Christians are called in general terms to both kinds of service, to witness to Christ and to play the good Samaritan when the opportunity presents itself, not all Christians are called either to give their lives to both or to spend all their spare time in both. It is clearly impossible for everybody to do everything which needs to be done. Therefore there must be specialization according to the gifts and calling of Christ. Some members of the local church are without doubt gifted for evangelism and called to evangelism. But can we now say with equal conviction that Christ's gifts and calling to others point rather in a social direction? Can we now liberate ourselves from the man-made bondage (for that is what it is) of supposing that every really keen Christian will devote all his spare time to some soul-winning enterprise? Surely the biblical doctrine of the body of Christ, with different members gifted to fulfil different functions, should be enough to give us this larger freedom?

Once this principle has been welcomed, it should be possible for groups of concerned Christians in every congregation to coalesce into a variety of 'study and action groups.' For example, one might concentrate on house-to-house visitation, another on the evangelistic penetration of some particular unreached section (*eg* a hostel or youth club, a college or coffee bar), another on community relations among immigrants, another on setting up a housing association to help the homeless, another on visiting old folk or the sick, or helping the handicapped, while others might address themselves to wider socio-ethical or socio-political questions such as abortion (if there is an abortion clinic in the parish) or labour relations (if the parish is industrial) or permissiveness and censorship (if local pornographic shops or cinemas are an offence in the neighbourhood). I have deliberately used the expression 'study and action groups' because we Christians have a tendency to pontificate from a position of ignorance, and we need to grapple with the complexities of our subject before recommending some course of responsible action, whether evangelistic or social or both, to the Church Council.

My third example of taking seriously the broader biblical understanding of mission brings us to the national scene. Although initiatives ought to be taken locally, it would be a considerable strength to parochial study and action groups if some kind of national network could be established. At the moment in England national organizations exist for youth work (*eg* Pathfinders and CYFA), for foreign missions (the various missionary societies), for overseas relief and development (*eg* TEAR Fund), and for one or two other purposes, but not for mission in the broader sense. The Church of England Evangelical Council and the Evangelical Alliance have begun talking about a 'think-tank' which might seek to develop a national strategy for the evangelization of Britain. I hope it will root itself in local situations by linking evangelistic 'study and action groups' with one another. Perhaps it should also be concerned not only for evangelism but for mission in the wider sense. Or maybe this is a job for the Shaftesbury Project or the Festival of Light or some other organization.

Out of such a network of local groups it seems to me that one or two influential central groups could arise. We hear a lot today about 'alienation,' not just in the classical economic sense developed by Marx, but in the more general sense of powerlessness. Jimmy Reid, the Marxist dockside leader who became Rector of Glasgow University in 1972, spoke about this during his installation address: 'Alienation is the cry of men who feel themselves to be the victims of blind economic forces beyond their control, . . . the frustration of ordinary people excluded from the processes of decision-making.' And it is true. Many people feel themselves to be helpless slaves of 'the system.' But Christians have no business to acquiesce in a feeling of helplessness. I find myself in agreement with Barbara Ward who, in what to me was the most scintillating speech at Uppsala, said: 'Christians straddle the whole spectrum of rich nations, and therefore Christians are a lobby, or can be a lobby, of incomprehensible importance . . .' She was talking particularly about development aid.

If we can accept this broader concept of mission as Christian service in the world comprising both evangelism and social action—a concept which is laid upon us by the model of our Saviour's mission in the world—then Christians could under God make a far greater impact on society, an impact commensurate with our numerical strength and with the radical demands of the commission of Christ.

2 Evangelism

The word 'mission,' I have so far suggested, is properly a comprehensive word, embracing everything which God sends his people into the world to do. It therefore includes evangelism and social responsibility, since both are authentic expressions of the love which longs to serve man in his need.

THE PRIORITY OF EVANGELISM

Yet I think we should agree with the statement of the Lausanne Covenant that 'in the church's mission of sacrificial service evangelism is primary' (para. 6 *The Church and Evangelism*). Christians should feel an acute pain of conscience and compassion when human beings are oppressed or neglected in any way, whether what is being denied them is civil liberty, racial respect, education, medicine, employment, or adequate food, clothing and shelter. Anything which undermines human dignity should be an offence to us. But is anything so destructive of human dignity as alienation from God through ignorance or rejection of the gospel? And how can we seriously maintain that political and economic liberation is just as important as eternal salvation? Both are certainly challenges to Christian love. But listen to the apostle Paul when he writes with solemn emphasis about his concern for his fellow Jews: 'I am speaking the truth in Christ, I am not lying; my conscience bears me witness in the Holy Spirit, that I have great sorrow and unceasing anguish in my heart. For I could wish that I myself were accursed and cut off from Christ for the sake of my brethren, my kinsmen by race' (Romans 9:1-3). What was the cause of his anguish? That they had lost their national Jewish independence and were under the colonial heel of Rome? That they were often despised and hated by Gentiles, socially boycoted and deprived of equal opportunities? No. 'Brethren, my heart's desire and prayer to God for them is that they may be saved' (Romans 10:1), and the context makes it plain beyond doubt that the 'salvation' Paul desired for them was their acceptance with God (vv2–4). That few if any of us feel this inward agony is a mark of our spiritual immaturity.

Moreover, in our evangelistic concern our chief burden should be for those whom Peter Wagner of the Fuller School of World Mission and Institute of Church Growth calls 'the Fourth World,' namely the more than 2,700 million unreached peoples of the world. In relation to them the Lausanne Covenant says: 'We are ashamed that so many have been neglected; it is a standing rebuke to us and to the whole church.' This is an echo of what John R. Mott said in connection with the great World Missionary Conference at Edinburgh in 1910. In his book *The Decisive Hour of Christian Missions*, written before he left Edinburgh and also of course before the Edinburgh euphoria had been shattered four years later by the first World War, he referred to the millions of non-Christian people in the world: 'It is the church's duty to see that this long-standing reproach is completely removed. Its plan of work, to be adequate, must provide for the evangelisation of the whole of this multitude.'

After the second World War, Bishop Stephen Neill was one of those who tried to keep evangelism at the heart of the ecumenical movement. In the book entitled *The Church's Witness to God's Design*, which was published in preparation for the Amsterdam Assembly in 1948 at which the World Council of Churches officially came into being, he wrote: 'The problem of the Church's mission is the crisis of the ecumenical movement. If an ecumenical movement is not primarily a strategy of worldwide evangelism, then it is nothing but an interesting academic exercise.' Dr Philip Potter told the Central Committee of the World Council at Crete in August 1967 that the wcc had been 'haunted' by these words. The integration of the International Missionary Council with the World Council of Churches at New Delhi in 1961 was intended to make evangelism central to ecumenical concern, but few would claim that this intention succeeded. Although the Bangkok call for a 'moratorium'—or temporary suspension—of missionary men and money was partially misunderstood, the impression was undoubtedly given that the WCC was, to say the least, no longer enthusiastic about the missionary task of the church. The Lausanne Covenant itself affirmed that 'a reduction of foreign missionaries and money in an evangelized country may sometimes be necessary,' but it added that the only reasons for such a drastic step would be 'to facilitate the national church's growth in self-reliance and to release resources for unevangelized areas.' It would not be to reduce missionary outreach. On the contrary, it went on—'Missionaries should flow ever more freely from and to all six continents in a spirit of humble service' (para. 9 *The Urgency of the Evangelistic Task*).

THE MEANING OF EVANGELISM

Granted, then, the priority of evangelism, how is it to be defined? In a few words, *euangelizomai* means to bring or to announce the *euangelion*, the good news. Once or twice in the New Testament it is used of ordinary, one might almost say 'secular' news items, as when the angel Gabriel told Zechariah the good news that his wife Elizabeth was to have a son (Luke 1:19), and when Timothy brought Paul the good news of the Thessalonians' faith and love (1 Thessalonians 3:6). The regular use of the verb relates, however, to the *Christian* good news. It is the spread of the gospel which constitutes evangelism, and this fact enables us to begin negatively by stating what evangelism is not.

First, evangelism must not be defined in terms of the *recipients* of the gospel, although it is of course assumed that they will be sufficiently 'non-Christian' to need to hear it. It was fashionable some years ago to distinguish between 'mission' and 'evangelism' by suggesting that mission is directed to those who have never heard the gospel, whereas evangelism concerns people in Christendom. But no, all who have not been reborn in Christ, whether they have heard the gospel or not, whether even they have been baptized or not, need to be 'evangelized,' *ie* they need to hear, or hear better, the good news. Dr Ralph Winter, another faculty member of the School of World Mission at Fuller Seminary, has distinguished between three kinds of evangelism, 'E-1,' 'E-2' and 'E-3' evangelism. E-1 evangelism is sharing the gospel with others of the same language and culture as oneself. E-2 evangelism is seeking to reach people of a similar language or culture, while E-3 evangelism is a cross-cultural activity. (*Let the Earth Hear His Voice*, the official reference volume of the ICOWE, 1975.) This is a helpful distinction, which takes the cultural factor in evangelism seriously. But notice that Dr Winter rightly calls all three activities 'evangelism.'

Secondly, evangelism must not be defined in terms of *results*, for this is not how the word is used in the New Testament. Normally the verb is in the middle voice. Occasionally it is used absolutely, for example 'there they evangelized,' meaning 'there they preached the gospel' (Acts 14:7 *cf* Romans 15:20). Usually, however, something is added. Sometimes it is the message they preached, *eg* they 'went about evangelizing the word' (Acts 8:4), while Philip in Samaria 'evangelized concerning the kingdom of God and the name of Jesus Christ' (Acts 8:12). Sometimes, however, what is added is the people to whom or the places in which the gospel was preached. For example, the apostles 'evangelized many villages of the Samaritans' and Philip 'evangelized all the towns' along the Palestinian coast (Acts 8:25, 40). There is no mention in these verses whether the word which was 'evangelized' was believed, or whether the inhabitants of the towns and villages 'evangelized' were converted. To 'evangelize' in New Testament usage does not mean to win converts, as it usually does when we use the word. Evangelism is the announcement of the good news, irrespective of the results.

You may recall that the famous watchword of the Student Volunteer Movement 'the evangelization of the world in this generation' was criticized for this reason. Professor Gustav Warneck attacked it at the 9th Continental Missions Conference at Bremen in May 1897, on the ground that it was a naïvely optimistic and rather man-confident forecast that the world would be won for Christ in that generation. But John Mott rallied to the watchword's defence. He maintained that 'the evangelization of the world' meant neither its conversion nor its Christianization, that it did not encourage superficial preaching and that it was not to be regarded as a prophecy (*The Evangelization of the World in this Generation*, John Mott, 1901, quoted by Hans Hoekendijk in the *International Review of Missions*, No. 233). As William Richey Hogg writes in his *Ecumenical Foundations* (Harper, 1952), the watchword was 'a call to obligation, not a prophecy of fact.'

Yet a number of definitions of evangelism have unashamedly included a reference to conversion. Kagawa said 'evangelism means the conversion of people from worldliness to Christlike godliness.' William Temple said that 'evangelism is the winning of men to acknowledge Christ as their Saviour and King, so that they may give themselves to his service in the fellowship of his Church.' The Evanston Assembly in 1954 spoke of evangelism as 'the bringing of persons to Christ as Saviour and Lord that they may share in his eternal life.' But evangelism is neither to convert people, nor to win them, nor to bring them to Christ, though this is indeed the first goal of evangelism. Evangelism is to preach the gospel.

Dr J. I. Packer in his essay *Evangelism and the Sovereignty of God* (IVP, 1961) has justly criticized the famous definition of evangelism first formulated in England in 1919 by the Archbishops' 'Committee of Enquiry into the Evangelistic Work of the Church.' It begins: 'to evangelize is so to present Christ Jesus in the power of the Holy Spirit that men shall come to put their trust in God through him . . .' Dr Packer draws attention to the form of the sentence '*so* to present Christ Jesus . . . that men shall . . .' This is to define evangelism in terms of success. But to evangelize is not *so* to preach that something happens. 'The way to tell whether in fact you are evangelizing is not to ask whether conversions are known to have resulted from your witness. It is to ask whether you are faithfully making known the gospel message.' He adds 'the results of preaching depend not on the wishes and intentions of men, but on the will of God Almighty.' Now of course our objective is that something *will* happen, namely that people will respond and believe. That is why we plead with them to 'be reconciled with God' (2 Corinthians 5:20). At the same time we must not confuse an objective (what we want to happen) with a consequence (what actually does happen). If we want to be biblically accurate we must insist that the essence of evangelism lies in the faithful proclamation of the gospel. It is with a view to persuasion indeed. We are not indifferent to results. We long for people to be converted. But it is still evangelism whether in fact men are persuaded to embrace it or not. I shall say more about the element of 'persuasion' later.

Thirdly, evangelism must not be defined in terms of *methods*. To evangelize is to announce the good news, however the announcement is made. It is to bring the good news, by whatever means it is brought. In different degrees we can evangelize by word of mouth (whether to individuals, groups or crowds); by print, picture or screen; by drama (whether what is dramatized is fact or fiction); by good works of love (Matthew 5:16); by a Christ-centred home; by a transformed life; and even by an almost speechless excitement about Jesus. Nevertheless, because evangelism is fundamentally an announcement, some verbalization is necessary if the content of the good news is to be communicated with any precision.

After these negatives, we come back to the positive statement that evangelism may and must be defined only in terms of *the message*. Therefore biblical evangelism makes the biblical evangel indispensable. Nothing hinders evangelism today more than the widespread loss of confidence in the truth, relevance and power of the gospel. When this ceases to be good news from God and becomes instead 'rumours of God' (Peter Berger's *Rumour of Angels* Allen Lane later Penguin, 1968) we can hardly expect the church to exhibit much evangelistic enthusiasm. Paul said he was 'eager' to preach the gospel in Rome. But then he was convinced that it was God's power for salvation (Romans 1:14–16).

IS THERE A NEW TESTAMENT GOSPEL?

What, then, is the New Testament gospel? Before we are in a position to answer this question two preliminary problems stand in our way. First, is there in fact one New Testament gospel? Are there not many? It is well known that the last-century Tübingen school based much of their interpretation of the New Testament on a supposed fundamental disagreement between Peter and Paul, and in more recent days the tendency of some scholars has been to discover a number of viewpoints all to some degree at variance with each other.

The New Testament certainly presents us with no wooden and unbending stereotype. There are clear differences of emphasis, owing to the author's own background and temperament, and to the Holy Spirit's revelation, so that the apostle Paul can dare to write of 'my gospel' when he is referring to the particular 'mystery' which has been disclosed to him.

There is also some historical development, even in the same author, so that what Paul writes in his later letters is recognizably different from what he has written earlier. Different situations also called forth different treatments. The apostolic approach was 'situational,' that is, a sensitive response to each particular challenge. Paul's synagogue sermon in Antioch diverged widely from his Areopagus address in Athens; so did his letter to the Romans from those to the Corinthians. Nevertheless, having allowed for all these variations, and despite all the rich diversity of theological formulation in the New Testament, there was only one basic apostolic tradition of the gospel. Paul insists to the Galatians that the Jerusalem apostles had given him 'the right hand of fellowship' as a sign of their acknowledgement of his mission and message (Galatians 1,2 esp. 2:9). In the same chapters he affirms vehemently that there is no other gospel, and calls down the curse of God upon anybody, angelic or apostolic—indeed even himself—who should presume to preach a different gospel. Later, in 1 Corinthians, after summarizing the gospel and listing the resurrection appearances, he concludes: 'Whether then it was I or they, so we preach and so you believed' (1 Corinthians 15:11). This cluster of personal pronouns—I, they, we and you—is very impressive. It is an assertion that he and the Jerusalem apostles were agreed about the gospel, that together the whole apostolic band proclaimed it, and that together the whole Christian church received and believed it. There is only one gospel.

The second preliminary question is whether the one New Testament gospel is transient because it was culturally conditioned, or whether it is changeless. There can be no gainsaying the fact that in the purpose of God his revelation reached its culmination in the first century AD, in Christ and in the apostolic witness to Christ, and therefore in what to us is an ancient culture of mixed Hebrew, Greek and Roman ingredients. Nor can there be any doubt that, in order to grasp his revelation, we have to think ourselves back into that culture. But the fact that God disclosed himself in terms of a particular culture gives us not a justification for rejecting his revelation, but rather the right principle by which to interpret it, and also the solemn responsibility to re-interpret it in terms meaningful to our own culture. But there is only one gospel, and in its essence it never changes.

Let me say something more about revelation and culture. I am arguing that evangelism must be defined in terms of the message which we share with others. We have good news to communicate. So if evangelism is to take place, there must be communication—a true communication between ancient revelation and modern culture. This means that our message must be at the same time, faithful and contemporary. First it must be faithful—faithful, that is, to Scripture. We find our message first and foremost not in any existential situation, but in the Bible. Dr Visser't Hooft, in an article entitled *Evangelism in the neopagan situation* wrote:

I do not believe that evangelism is adequately described as answering the questions which men are asking, however deep those questions may be. For evangelism is in the first place the transmission of God's question to man. And that question is and remains whether we are willing to accept Jesus Christ as the one and only Lord of Life.

'International Review of Mission,' Vol. LXIII, No. 249, Jan. 1974

But he goes on to say that we must 'try to relate God's question to the existential situation of men and show that as they answer God's question they find at the same time the answer to their deepest concerns.'

Now it is comparatively easy to be faithful if we do not care about being contemporary, and easy also to be contemporary if we do not bother to be faithful. It is the search for a combination of truth and relevance which is exacting. Yet nothing else can save us from an insensitive loyalty to formulae and shibboleths on the one hand, and from a treasonable disloyalty to the revelation of God on the other. 'Truth and timeliness' (to quote Bishop Phillips Brooks) make for communication, and without communication there is no evangelism, no actual sharing of the good news.

We come back now to our earlier question: what is the one, the changeless New Testament gospel? And in stating it, can we indicate at all its contemporary power? The first and best answer would be to say that the whole Bible is God's good news in all its astonishing relevance. 'Bible' and 'gospel' are almost alternative terms, for the major function of the Bible in all its length and breadth is to bear witness to Jesus Christ. Nevertheless, God's revelation recorded in Scripture has been distilled for us in the good news the apostles proclaimed. What is it?

It is over 40 years since C. H. Dodd gave three lectures at King's College, London, which were later published under the title *The Apostolic Preaching and its Developments* (Hodder, 1936). His distinction between *kerygma* and *didache*, between the proclamation of the gospel and the ethical instruction of converts, has become well known. So has his reconstruction of the *kerygma* as preached by Paul and as contained in the speeches attributed to Peter in the Acts, and his recognition of a remarkable 'coincidence' between the two. All later reconstructions are in debt to C. H. Dodd, and it will readily be seen that mine is but a reshuffling of his cards, with the addition of a few he inadvertently omitted!

All concur that in a single word, God's good news is Jesus. On the Day of Pentecost, after quoting from Joel, Peter began his sermon proper: 'Men of Israel hear these

words: Jesus . . .' (Acts 2:22). His first word was Jesus, and
Jesus must be our first word too. Jesus Christ is the heart
and soul of the gospel. When Philip sat down beside the
Ethiopian, we are told literally that 'he evangelized to
him Jesus,' that is, he shared with him the good news of
Jesus (Acts 8:35). Similarly Paul began his great mani-
festo to the Romans by describing himself as 'set apart for
the gospel of God . . . concerning his Son . . . Jesus Christ
our Lord' (Romans 1:1–4). And we must all be
profoundly thankful that the personality of Jesus retains
its powerful hold over the minds of men. Hindus and
Moslems, Marxist revolutionaries, orthodox Jews and the
youthful counterculture of the West—all feel his fascination; none can escape his spell.

But how did the apostles present Jesus? Their good
news contained at least five elements.

THE GOSPEL EVENTS

First, of course, there were *the gospel events*. For certain
'things' had 'happened' in Jerusalem and 'been accomplished' among them (Luke 1:1, 24:14, 18), which nobody
could deny. In particular, Jesus of Nazareth had been
crucified and resurrected. So Paul summarizes the gospel
tradition: 'I delivered to you as of first importance what I
also received, that Christ died for our sins . . ., that he was
buried, that he was raised on the third day . . ., and that
he appeared . . .' (1 Corinthians 15:3, 4, 5). He actually
mentions four events—the death, burial, resurrection and
appearance of Jesus. Yet it is clear that his emphasis is on
two, namely that Christ died (and was buried in order
to prove it) and that Christ rose (and was seen in order
to prove it). The appearance attested the reality of his
resurrection, as the burial attested the reality of his
death.

The same stress on the resurrection of Jesus is clear in
the speeches of the Acts. Sometimes the apostle Peter
would begin with a reference to the life and ministry of
the man Jesus (Acts 2:23, 3:22, 10:36–39 *cf* 13:23–25), and
sometimes he went on to his exaltation, reign and return.
But Peter's message like Paul's focused on Jesus's death
and resurrection. Both events were real, objective and

historical. And surely the right response to the existential mood of today is not to create a parallel Christian existentialism which despises history in favour of experience, and demythologizes the resurrection into an inward encounter with reality, but rather to offer to the modern mind as it flounders in the quicksands of subjectivity the objective bedrock of Jesus Christ whose death and resurrection are solid historical events.

The apostles did not present their Lord's death and resurrection merely as historical events, however, but as significant events, as saving events. Paul was clear that 'he died for our sins' (1 Corinthians 15:3 *cf* Galatians 1:4) and was 'raised for our justification' (Romans 4:25). It is sometimes said that, by contrast, the apostle Peter in his early Acts speeches had no doctrine of the cross, but proclaimed it as untheological history. This is C. H. Dodd's position, for example (*op. cit.*). Yet one wonders if he allows sufficiently for the implications of what Peter said. First he attributed the cross as much to 'the definite plan and foreknowledge of God' as to 'the hands of lawless men' (Acts 2:23), and if the cross was part of a divine purpose, it must have had a meaning. Secondly, he designated Jesus God's 'servant,' which must be an allusion to the suffering servant who bore the sins of many (Acts 3:13; 4:27 *cf* 8:32, 33). Thirdly, there is the surprising description of the crucifixion as a 'hanging' of Jesus on a 'tree' (Acts 5:30; 10:39 *cf* 13:29). This example of apostolic shorthand looked back to Deuteronomy 21:23, which said that any man hanged on a tree was under the curse of God, and so also anticipated the developed doctrine of Christ bearing our sin and even the curse of the law, which we find later in the letters of both Paul and Peter (Galatians 3:10, 13 and 1 Peter 2:24).

Certainly too the resurrection was more than a historical event. It was a divine vindication of Jesus. 'You killed him,' Peter repeated several times (Acts 2:23, 24; 3:15; 5:30, 31), 'but God raised him,' thus reversing the verdict of men, snatching him from the place of a curse and exalting him to his own right hand as Lord, Christ and Saviour (Acts 2:23, 24; 3:13–15; 5:30, 31).

THE GOSPEL WITNESSES

The second element in the apostles' message is *the gospel witnesses*, by which I mean the evidence to which they appealed for its authentication. This was twofold, in order that in the mouth of two witnesses the truth of the testimony might be established. The first was the Old Testament Scriptures. Paul emphasized this by repetition in his succinct statement of the gospel (1 Corinthians 15:3, 4): 'Christ died for our sins in accordance with the Scriptures . . .' and 'was raised on the third day in accordance with the Scriptures.' And Peter kept quoting Scripture in his Acts speeches, to demonstrate that the Christ of Old Testament expectation was Jesus. Surely we can say with confidence that this truth of the fulfilment of Scripture in his death and resurrection the apostles had learned from Jesus himself, partly during his public ministry, but especially after his resurrection, as Luke records? They would never forget his words, that 'everything written about me in the law of Moses and the prophets and the psalms must be fulfilled.' Then he opened their minds to understand the Scriptures, and said to them: 'Thus it is written, that the Christ should suffer and on the third day rise from the dead . . .' (Luke 24:44*ff*). In this way the apostles urged that they were not innovators. They had not invented their message. As Paul was to claim later, when standing on trial before Agrippa: 'So I stand here testifying both to small and great, saying nothing but what the prophets and Moses said would come to pass: that the Christ must suffer, and that, by being the first to rise from the dead, he would proclaim light to the people and to the Gentiles' (Acts 26:22, 23).

The emphasis upon Scripture had another significance. Since the death of Jesus, his resurrection, and his subsequent outpouring of the Spirit were all in fulfilment of Messianic prophecy, it was evident that the new age had dawned and that Christ had ushered it in. As C. H. Dodd puts it: 'The Pauline *kerygma* . . . is a proclamation of the facts of the death and resurrection of Christ in an eschatological setting which gives significance to the facts,' indeed a 'saving significance' (*op. cit.*).

But the Scriptures were only the first witness to the

events; there was a second. This was the evidence of the
apostles' own eyes. Jesus himself had linked the forthcom-
ing apostolic witness to the prophetic witness of the Old
Testament when he added to his reference to Scripture
'you are witnesses of these things' (Luke 24:48). He did it
again before the Ascension: 'you shall be my witnesses'
(Acts 1:8). They knew they were uniquely qualified to
witness to Christ, not just because they had been 'with
him from the beginning' (*cf* Mark 3:14; John 15:26; Acts
1:21, 22), but specially because they had seen the cross
and the risen Christ with their own eyes. So Peter
regularly included in his sermons a reference to the apostolic witness:

This Jesus God raised up, and of that we all are witnesses.

Acts 2:32

You . . . killed the Author of life, whom God raised from the
dead. To this we are witnesses.

Acts 3:15

And we are witnesses to these things.

Acts 5:32

To Cornelius Peter was even more explicit:

And we are witnesses to all that he did both in the country of the
Jews and in Jerusalem. They put him to death by hanging him
on a tree; but God raised him on the third day and made him
manifest; not to all the people but to us who were chosen by God
as witnesses, who ate and drank with him after he rose from the
dead. And he commanded us to preach to the people, and to
testify . . .

Acts 10:39–42

Thus the apostles joined together the witness of the Old
Testament prophets and their own witness, which came
later to be recorded in the New Testament.

The importance for our own day of this double authentication is not far to seek. We have already noted the
fascination which the person of Jesus has for our contemporaries, and that this often gives us a meeting point with
them. But which Jesus are we talking about? Even Paul in
his day recognized the possibility of teachers proclaiming
'another Jesus' than the Jesus he preached (2 Corinthians
11:4). And there are many Jesuses abroad today. There is
Jesus the Bultmannian myth and Jesus the revolutionary
firebrand, Jesus the failed superstar and Jesus the circus

clown. It is over against these human reinterpretations that we need urgently to recover and reinstate the authentic Jesus, the Jesus of history who is the Jesus of Scripture.

This means, further, that we have no liberty to preach Jesus Christ according to our own fantasy, or even according to our own experience. Our personal witness does indeed corroborate the witness of the biblical authors, especially that of the apostles. But theirs is the primary witness, for they were 'with Jesus' and knew him, and they have borne witness to what they heard with their ears and saw with their eyes. Our witness is always secondary and subordinate to theirs. So there is no escape from the continuing work of conservative scholars who are seeking to defend the reliability of the gospel portrait of Jesus and to re-establish public confidence in the apostolic witness. Our responsibility in evangelism is neither to create a Christ of our own who is not in Scripture, nor to embroider or manipulate the Christ who is in Scripture, but to bear faithful witness to the one and only Christ there is as God has presented him to the world in the remarkably unified testimony of both the Old and the New Testament Scriptures.

THE GOSPEL AFFIRMATIONS

Thirdly, there were and still are *the gospel affirmations*. When David Anderson was Principal of Wycliffe Hall, he wrote in 1966 to former students about a conference at which the teaching and preaching of doctrine had been discussed. Many were saying that 'the days of authoritarian sermons had now passed' and that 'we must present the Gospel in terms acceptable to the questioning temper of our age.'

But [*David Anderson continued*] Basil Mitchell [*one of our Oxford philosophers*] dissented from this view. When he went to church, he said, he wanted to hear a word of real authority from the preacher, and not just a lot of qualified propositions. The word of the Lord is a word from God and a word about God: it is not a word of human opinion, and the preacher is not doing his job if he is failing to present to his people the great affirmations of the Gospel.

What, then, are the gospel affirmations? As we have

seen, they centre on Jesus Christ. They concern not simply what he *did* more than nineteen centuries ago, however, but what he *is* today in consequence. The historical Christ is the contemporary Christ. In New Testament terms, the fundamental affirmation is that 'Jesus is Lord.' If we confess with our lips that 'Jesus is Lord,' Paul wrote, and believe in our heart that God raised him from the dead, we will be saved (Romans 10:9). Indeed, the end for which Christ died and rose again was 'that he might be Lord both of the dead and of the living' (Romans 14:9). For God has highly exalted Jesus and bestowed on him the name above every name that every knee should bow to him and every tongue confess that 'Jesus Christ is Lord' (Philippians 2:9–11). It is an essentially Christian affirmation, for no one can make it but by the illumination of the Holy Spirit (1 Corinthians 12:3).

What Paul insists on in these texts is that the lordship or sovereignty of Jesus is a direct consequence of his death and resurrection. Peter taught the same in his Acts speeches. It is the Jesus who died and whom God raised up who is now 'exalted at the right hand of God' (Acts 2:32, 33, *cf* 3:13; 4:11). This was in fulfilment of the great Messianic promise 'Sit at my right hand, till I make your enemies your footstool' (Psalm 110:1), which not only looked back to the Saviour's completed work from which he was now resting, as the writer to the Hebrews shows (Hebrews 10:12), but also looks on to the final triumph for which he is now waiting. Yet this is assured. Already in anticipation, Peter could say to Cornelius, albeit in a parenthesis, 'he is Lord of all' (Acts 10:36).

The 'right hand of God' at which Christ 'sits' is then symbolic of his universal authority because of which he is able both to bestow blessing and to require submission. First, the blessing. It was after his exaltation to God's right hand that he 'received from the Father the promise of the Holy Spirit' and poured out on his church this distinctive blessing of the new age (Acts 2:33). According to the Joel prophecy which Peter said had been fulfilled, it was God himself who had promised 'I will pour out my Spirit upon all flesh' (v17). Yet, knowing this, Peter does not hesitate to attribute the outpouring to Jesus who occupies the position of supreme honour and authority at the Father's right hand.

If from the throne Jesus bestows blessing upon his people he also expects them to submit to him, to bow their knee to him. 'Let all the house of Israel therefore know assuredly that God has made him both Lord and Christ, this Jesus whom you crucified' (v36). These words formed the climax of Peter's sermon. They cut his listeners to the heart and made them cry out for instruction what to do. They must repent, Peter said. God had reversed their verdict on Jesus, for they had killed him but God had raised him. Now they must reverse their verdict too. They must bring the whole of life, individual and social, under the sovereign lordship of Jesus. To be in his kingdom or under his rule brings both total blessing and total demand.

Thus the symbolic statement that Jesus is 'at God's right hand' comprises the two great gospel affirmations that he is Saviour (with authority to bestow salvation) and that he is Lord (with authority to demand submission). The two are joined by Peter in his second speech to the Sanhedrin: 'God exalted him at his right hand as Leader and Saviour, to give repentance to Israel and forgiveness of sins' (Acts 5:31).

Moreover, both affirmations are part of the absolute uniqueness of Jesus Christ. If we are asked in today's increasingly syncretistic culture wherein lies the uniqueness of Jesus, I think we should have to answer 'Jesus is Lord' and 'Jesus is Saviour'. Theologically speaking, these affirmations express the great doctrines of incarnation and atonement, and there is nothing comparable to them in the ethnic religions. The claimed 'avatars' ('descents' or so-called 'incarnations') of Hinduism not only lack historical foundation but their incidental nature and their plurality set them apart from the central Christian claim that once only and in verifiable history God became man in Jesus. And the repeated promises in the Koran of the forgiveness of a compassionate and merciful Allah are all made to the meritorious, whose merits have been weighed in Allah's scales, whereas the gospel is good news of mercy to the undeserving. The symbol of the religion of Jesus is the cross, not the scales. The world is still waiting to hear these gospel affirmations, and to hear them in the present tense which speaks to men today, namely 'Jesus is Lord' and 'Jesus is Saviour.'

THE GOSPEL PROMISES

Fourthly, we turn logically from the gospel affirmations to *the gospel promises*, to what Christ now offers and indeed promises to those who come to him. For the good news concerns neither just what Jesus once *did* (he died and rose again), not just what he now *is* (exalted to God's right hand as Lord and Saviour) but also what he now *offers* as a result. What is this? At the end of his Pentecost sermon Peter promised the crowd with great assurance that if they repented and were baptized they would receive two free gifts of God, namely 'the forgiveness of sins' and 'the gift of the Holy Spirit.'

Forgiveness is an essential ingredient of the salvation offered in the gospel. The risen Lord had commanded that 'remission of sins' be proclaimed to all nations on the basis of his name (Luke 24:47), and the reformed understanding of his statement 'if you forgive the sins of any, they are forgiven' (John 20:23) has always been that he was telling them to preach the terms of the divine forgiveness with boldness and authority. Certainly this is what the apostles did. 'Repent,' cried Peter, 'and turn again that your sins may be blotted out' (Acts 3:19). And he assured Cornelius: 'every one who believes in him receives forgiveness of sins through his name' (Acts 10:43). Similarly, Paul declared in the Antiochene synagogue: 'through this man forgiveness of sins is proclaimed to you' (Acts 13:38). However unpopular this message may be today, forgiveness remains man's chief need and an indispensable part of the good news.

But Christ offers more than the forgiveness of our past. He offers too a new life in the present through the regeneration and indwelling of the Holy Spirit, who is also the guarantee of our future inheritance in heaven. We must not separate the two gospel promises which God has joined together, forgiveness and the Spirit. Both belong to the 'salvation' which Peter insisted was in Jesus Christ

alone (Acts 4:12), and both are part of the 'liberation'
which modern man is now seeking. True freedom is more
than deliverance from guilt; it is deliverance also from self,
from what Malcolm Muggeridge calls 'the dark little dun-
geon of my own ego.' Once rescued from guilt and self-
centredness, we can give ourselves to the service of God
and man. And only in this servitude is true freedom to be
found.

THE GOSPEL DEMANDS

Fifthly, we come to *the gospel demands*. We move from what
Jesus did, is and promises, to what he requires of us
today. We have already seen that Peter's first word in
answer to the crowd's conscience-stricken question what
they should do was 'repent.' It was his first word again at
the conclusion of his second sermon: 'Repent therefore'
(Acts 3:19). And Paul ended his sermon to the Athenians
with the statement that God 'now commands all men
everywhere to repent' (Acts 17:30).

To repent was to turn from their sin, and in particular
their grievous sin of rejecting Jesus. Their *metanoia* or
'change of mind' was, then, a reversal of their opinion of
Jesus and of their attitude to him. They had repudiated
him and expressed their rejection in the crucifixion; now
they were to believe in him as Lord, Christ and Saviour,
and express their acceptance in their baptism. For,
although baptism no doubt means more than this, it cannot mean less. They were to be baptized 'in the name of
Jesus Christ.' That is, they were to submit humbly to
baptism in the name of the very person they had
previously sought to destroy. Nothing could indicate more
clearly than this their public and penitent faith in him.
Further, their repentance and baptism introduced them
into the new community of Jesus. There was no conversion without church membership, as I shall argue at
greater length in Chapter 5.

The speaker at Lausanne who laid greatest emphasis on
the indispensable necessity of repentance was Dr René
Padilla from Argentina. He also insisted on the social
dimension of repentance. In that section of his pre-
Congress paper which was entitled 'Evangelism and

repentance ethics' he wrote: 'This new reality (*sc.* the arrival of the Kingdom) places men in a position of crisis—they cannot continue to live as if nothing had happened; the Kingdom of God demands a new mentality, a reorientation of all their values, repentance.' Also, 'the change imposed involves a new life-style . . . Without ethics there is no real repentance . . . And without repentance there is no salvation.' Further, 'Repentance is much more than a private affair between the individual and God. It is the complete reorientation of life in the world—among men—in response to the work of God in Jesus Christ' (*Let the Earth Hear His Voice*, Worldwide Publications, 1974.

Thus social responsibility becomes an aspect not of Christian mission only, but also of Christian conversion. It is impossible to be truly converted to God (as we shall consider in the last chapter) without being thereby converted to our neighbour.

Conversion includes faith as well as repentance. It is true that Peter's command to the crowd was to 'repent' rather than to 'believe.' Yet, those who received Peter's word, repented and were baptized are a few verses later referred to as 'believers' (Acts 2:44). 'Everyone who believes in him receives forgiveness,' Peter said to Cornelius (Acts 10:43). 'Believe in the Lord Jesus and you will be saved,' Paul said to the jailer at Philippi (Acts 16:31).

So the gospel demands are repentance and faith—and (in public) baptism. This leads me to mention a controversy in certain evangelical circles. Some have been so determined to maintain the doctrine of justification by faith alone that they have not been able to accommodate themselves to the addition of repentance. They distinguish sharply between the acceptance of Jesus as Saviour and the surrender to him as Lord, and they even promulgate the grotesque notion that to insist on surrender in addition to acceptance is to distort the gospel. Well, I honour their conscientious desire to protect the gospel from all perversions. And certainly justification is by grace alone in Christ alone through faith alone. Further, we must be careful never to define faith in such a way as to ascribe to it any merit. The whole value of faith lies in its object (Jesus Christ), not in itself. Nevertheless, saving faith is not an 'acceptance of Jesus Christ as Saviour' within a kind of mystical vacuum and without any awareness either of the Christ being 'accepted' or of the concrete implications of this acceptance. Saving faith is a total, penitent and submissive commitment to Christ, and it would have been inconceivable to the apostles that anybody could believe in Jesus as Saviour without submitting to him as Lord. We have already seen that the one exalted to God's right hand is Jesus the Lord and Saviour. We cannot chop this Jesus into bits and then respond to only one of the bits. The object of saving faith is the whole and undivided person of our Lord and Saviour, Jesus Christ.

One other point before I leave the gospel demands. We must not miss the note of urgency as well as authority in which the apostles issued their call to repent and believe. They were conscious not only that the summons came from the throne where Jesus reigned but also that this same Jesus would return as Judge. The God who 'now . . . commands all men everywhere to repent' had already fixed the judgment day and appointed the Judge. He is Jesus, the same one who had died and been resurrected (Acts 17:30, 31 *cf* 3:20, 21; 10:42; 13:40, 41).

THE CONTEXT OF EVANGELISM

Evangelism, then, is sharing the good news with others. The good news is Jesus. And the good news about Jesus which we announce is that he died for our sins and was raised from death, and that in consequence he reigns as Lord and Saviour at God's right hand, and has authority both to command repentance and faith, and to bestow forgiveness of sins and the gift of the Spirit on all those who repent, believe and are baptized. And all this is according to the Scriptures of the Old and New Testaments. It is more than that. It is precisely what is meant by 'proclaiming the Kingdom of God.' For in fulfilment of Scripture God's reign has broken into the life of men through the death and resurrection of Jesus. This reign or rule of God is exercised from the throne by Jesus, who bestows salvation and requires obedience. These are the blessing and the demand of the Kingdom. As Jesus himself had put it at the very beginning of his public ministry: 'The time is fulfilled, and the Kingdom of God is at hand; repent and believe in the gospel' (Mark 1:15).

Finally, having tried to define evangelism in terms of the evangel, I think I need to say something about its context, for the proclamation of the gospel cannot be seen as an activity in isolation. Something precedes it and something follows it. What precedes it may justly be called 'presence' and what follows it 'persuasion.' Peter Wagner in his book *Frontiers in Missionary Strategy* (Moody, 1971) has popularized what he calls '3-P evangelism' consisting of these three words 'presence, proclamation and persuasion.' Although I am not myself happy to include all three in a strict definition of evangelism itself, yet presence must certainly precede evangelism, as persuasion must follow it.

The notion of the 'Christian presence' has not always commended itself because its advocates have sometimes spoken of a 'silent presence' or an 'authentic silence.' No doubt there are occasions when it is more Christian to be silent than to speak. Yet the Christian presence in the world is intended by God to lead to the Christian proclamation to the world. At the same time we have to concede with shame that the ecumenical emphasis on silence is at least partly a justifiable reaction against some of our brash and aggressive evangelical forms of evangelism. If, however, generally speaking, there should be no presence without proclamation, we must equally assert that there should be no proclamation without presence. The risen Lord's first word of commission was not 'preach' but 'go.' And going into the world means presence.

Moreover, it is to be the visible presence of a church which bears an attractive aspect. As Samuel Escobar wrote in his paper for the Lausanne Congress: 'The primitive church was not perfect, but evidently it was a community that called the attention of men because of the qualitative differences of its life. The message was not only heard from them, it was also seen in the way they lived' (*Let the Earth Hear His Voice*). There can be no evangelism without the church. The message comes from a community which embodies it and which welcomes into its fellowship those who receive it. This fact immediately brings a challenge to the church. Dr Visser't Hooft in 1949 referred to the 'boomerang effect' of the evangelistic question:

> The Church which would call the world to order is suddenly called to order itself. The question which it would throw into the world: 'Do you know that you belong to Christ?' comes back as an echo. The Church discovers that it cannot truly evangelize, that its message is unconvincing unless it lets itself be transformed and renewed, unless it becomes what it believes it is.
>
> *Quoted by Philip Potter in his 1967 address to the WCC central committee in Crete*

The other word is 'persuasion.' I mentioned earlier J. I. Packer's criticism of the Archbishops' definition of evangelism. Peter Wagner has now criticized Jim Packer's criticism, and wants to insist that persuasion is itself a part of evangelism. In answer, we must certainly accept that Paul described his evangelistic preaching by the statement 'we persuade men' (2 Corinthians 5:11), and that many times in the Acts Luke describes him doing so, adding that many were 'persuaded.' This is not in dispute, but to make the persuasion of men a part of our definition of evangelism is to confuse the activity itself with its goals. Our goal is indeed 'so to present Christ Jesus in the power of the Holy Spirit' that men may be persuaded to come to him in penitence. The World Congress on Evangelism at Berlin in 1966 correctly declared that 'evangelism is the proclamation of the gospel . . . with the purpose of persuading lost and condemned sinners to put their trust in God. . . .' We have this liberty to state our purpose: yet it is not for us to determine the *issue*. Some speak of 'persuasion' as if the outcome could be secured by human effort, almost as if it were another word for 'coercion.' But no. Our responsibility is to be faithful; the results are in the hand of Almighty God.

I do not think I can conclude more appropriately than by quoting paragraph 4 of the Lausanne Covenant which is entitled *The Nature of Evangelism*:

> To evangelize is to spread the good news that Jesus Christ died for our sins and was raised from the dead according to the Scriptures, and that as the reigning Lord he now offers the

forgiveness of sins and the liberating gift of the Spirit to all who repent and believe. Our Christian presence in the world is in--dispensable to evangelism, and so is that kind of dialogue whose purpose is to listen sensitively in order to understand. But evangelism itself is the proclamation of the historical, biblical Christ as Saviour and Lord, with a view to persuading people to come to him personally and so be reconciled to God. In issuing the gospel invitation we have no liberty to conceal the cost of discipleship. Jesus still calls all who would follow him to deny themselves, take up their cross, and identify themselves with his new community. The results of evangelism include obedience to Christ, incorporation into his church and responsible service in the world.

3 Dialogue

My argument so far has been that 'mission' denotes the self-giving service which God sends his people into the world to render, and includes both evangelism and socio-political action; that within this broadly conceived mission a certain urgency attaches to evangelism, and priority must be given to it; and that 'evangelism' means announcing or proclaiming the good news of Jesus. This brings us to the third word 'dialogue,' and to the question: Is there any room for dialogue in the proclamation of the good news? It is well known that during the past decade or two the concept of 'dialogue with men of other faiths' has become the ecumenical fashion, and that evangelicals have tended to react rather sharply against it. Is our negative reaction justified? And what are the issues anyway?

EXTREME VIEWS
Extreme positions have been taken on both sides of this debate. Evangelical Christians have always—and in my judgment rightly—emphasized the indispensable necessity of preaching the gospel, for God has appointed his church to be the herald of the good news. An eloquent summons to proclamation has recently been issued by Dr Martyn Lloyd-Jones in his book *Preaching and Preachers* (Hodder and Stoughton, 1971). His first chapter is entitled 'The Primacy of Preaching,' and on its first page he writes: 'to me the work of preaching is the highest and the greatest and the most glorious calling to which anyone can ever be called. If you want something in addition to that I would say without any hesitation that the most urgent need in the Christian Church today is true preaching, and as it is

the greatest and most urgent need in the Church, it is obviously the greatest need for the world also.' Indeed, because man's essential trouble is his rebellion against God and his need of salvation, therefore 'preaching is the primary task of the Church.' To his passionate advocacy of preaching Dr Lloyd-Jones has sometimes added his distaste for the concept of dialogue: 'God is not to be discussed or debated . . . Believing what we do about God, we cannot in any circumstances allow Him to become a subject for discussion or debate or investigation . . . as if He were but a philosophical proposition.'

And the same goes for the gospel: the gospel is suitable for proclamation, not for amiable discussion. Now if by 'discussion' we have in mind the work of clever diplomats at the conference table, whose objective is to satisfy (even appease) everybody, and whose method is to reach consensus by compromise, I find myself in whole-hearted agreement with Dr Lloyd-Jones. The gospel is a nonnegotiable revelation from God. We may certainly discuss its meaning and its interpretation, so long as our purpose is to grasp it more firmly ourselves and commend it more acceptably to others. But we have no liberty to sit in judgment on it, or to tamper with its substance. For it is God's gospel not ours, and its truth is to be received not criticized, declared not discussed. Having said this, however, it is necessary to add that, properly understood, 'dialogue' and 'discussion' are two different things.

At the other extreme there is a growing dislike for preaching, or at least for preaching of an authoritative or dogmatic kind. Proclamation is said to be arrogant; the humble way of communication is the way of dialogue. It would be difficult to find a more articulate exponent of this view than Professor J. G. Davies of Birmingham. In his small book *Dialogue with the World* (SCM, 1967) he writes: 'Monologue is entirely lacking in humility: it assumes that we know all and that we merely have to declare it, to pass it on to the ignorant, whereas we need to seek truth together, that our truth may be corrected and deepened as it encounters the truths of those with whom we are in dialogue.' Further, 'monologue . . . is deficient in openness,' whereas 'dialogue involves complete openness.' Professor Davies goes on:

To enter into dialogue in this way is not only difficult, it is dangerous. Complete openness means that every time we enter into dialogue our faith is at stake. If I engage in dialogue with a Buddhist and do so with openness I must recognize that the outcome cannot be predetermined either for him or for me. The Buddhist may come to accept Jesus as Lord, but I may come to accept the authority of the Buddha, or even both of us may end up as agnostics. Unless these are *real* possibilities, neither of us is being fully open to the other . . . To live dialogically is to live dangerously . . .

For myself I regard this as an intemperate over-statement. It is true that good Christian preaching is always dialogical, in the sense that it engages the minds of the listeners and speaks to them with relevance. But it is not true to say that all monologue is proud. The evangelist who proclaims the gospel is not claiming to 'know all,' but only to have been put in trust with the gospel. We should also, as I believe and shall soon argue, be willing to enter into dialogue. In doing so we shall learn from the other person both about his beliefs and also (by listening to his critical reaction to Christianity) about certain aspects of our own. But we should not cultivate a total 'openness' in which we suspend even our convictions concerning the truth of the gospel and our personal commitment to Jesus Christ. To attempt to do this would be to destroy our own integrity as Christians.

DIALOGUE IN THE BIBLE
In this dialogue about dialogue, perhaps the place to begin is with definition. A more simple and straightforward definition I have not found than that framed at the National Evangelical Anglican Congress held at Keele in 1967: 'Dialogue is a conversation in which each party is serious in his approach both to the subject and to the other person, and desires to listen and learn as well as to speak and instruct' (para. 83).

After this definition it is important to note that the living God of the biblical revelation himself enters into a dialogue with man. He not only speaks but listens. He

asks questions and waits for the answers. Ever since his
question went echoing among the trees of the garden of
Eden, 'Where are you?,' God has been seeking his fallen
creature, and addressing questions to him. Of course the
approach of the Infinite to the finite, of the Creator to the
creature, of the Holy to the sinful has always been one of
gracious self-disclosure. Nevertheless, the form his revelation has taken has often been dialogical. 'Gird up your
loins like a man,' he said to Job. 'I will question you, and
you shall declare to me, (Job 38:3; 40:7). And his address
to Israel through the prophets was full of questions.

Come now, let us reason together, says the Lord.
What wrong did your fathers find in me that they went far from
me. . . ?
Why do you complain against me?
Have you not known? Have you not heard?
Has it not been told you from the beginning?
Have you not understood from the foundations of the earth?
How can I give you up, O Ephraim!
How can I hand you over, O Israel!
Isaiah 1:18; Jeremiah 2:5, 29; Isaiah 40:21; Hosea 11:8

Jesus too, who himself as a boy was found in the temple
'sitting among the teachers listening to them and asking
them questions' (Luke 2:46), during his public ministry
entered into serious conversations with individuals like
Nicodemus, the Samaritan woman and the crowds. He
seldom if ever spoke in a declamatory, take-it-or-leave-it
style. Instead, whether explicitly or implicitly, he was
constantly addressing questions to his hearers' minds and
consciences. For example, 'When . . . the owner of the
vineyard comes, what will he do to those tenants?'
(Matthew 21:40). Again, 'which of these three, do you
think, proved neighbour to the man who fell among the
robbers?' (Luke 10:36). Even after the Ascension when he
revealed himself to Saul of Tarsus on the Damascus Road,
and the prostrate and blinded Pharisee appeared at first
to have been crushed by the vision, Jesus addressed him a
rational question: 'Why do you persecute me?' and
provoked the counterquestions, 'Who are you, Lord?' and
'What shall I do, Lord?' (Acts 9:4, 5; 22:10).

When later Saul began his great missionary journeys as

Paul the apostle, it is instructive to notice that some form
of dialogue was an integral part of his method. At least
Luke not infrequently uses the verb *dialegomai* to describe
an aspect of his evangelism, especially during the second
and third expeditions. True, there is some uncertainty
about the precise meaning of the verb. In classical Greek
it meant to 'converse' or 'discuss' and was particularly
associated with the so-called 'dialectic' as a means of
instruction and persuasion developed in different ways by
Socrates, Plato and Aristotle. In the Gospels it is once
used of the apostles' argumentative discussion with each
other who was the greatest (Mark 9:34). In reference to
Paul's ministry Gottlob Schrenk in Kittel's *Theological
Dictionary* (Eerdmans) says that it refers to the 'delivering
of religious lectures or sermons' but has no reference to
'disputation.' The Arndt-Gingrich lexicon, on the other
hand, though conceding that it sometimes means 'simply
to speak or preach' (*eg* Hebrews 12:5), maintains that it is
used 'of lectures which were likely to end in disputations.'
The context certainly suggests this too.

Thus in the synagogue at Thessalonica for three weeks
'Paul . . . argued with them from the Scriptures, explaining and proving that it was necessary for the Christ to
suffer and to rise from the dead, and saying "This Jesus,
whom I proclaim to you, is the Christ."' Luke then adds:
'some of them were persuaded' (Acts 17:1–4). Here five
words are brought together—arguing, explaining, proving, proclaiming and persuading—which suggest that
Paul was actually debating with the Jews, hearing and
answering their objections to his message. In Athens we
are told that he 'argued' both 'in the synagogue with the
Jews and the devout persons, and in the market place
every day with those who chanced to be there' (17:17).
This is an important addition because it shows that his
reasoning approach was with casual Gentile passers-by as
well as with Jews in the synagogue. In Corinth he 'argued
in the synagogue every sabbath and persuaded Jews and
Greeks' (18:4), while at Ephesus he first 'entered the
synagogue and for three months spoke boldly, arguing
and pleading about the kingdom of God' and then for two
years 'argued daily in the hall of Tyrannus' possibly for as

long as five hours a day (19:8–10 *cf* 18:19).

Paul also used the same method in Christian preaching, for during the famous 'breaking of bread' at Troas, during which the young man Eutychus fell asleep with nearly disastrous consequences, *dialegomai* is again used to describe Paul's address (Acts 20:7, 9). The last example is also interesting, because we find Paul having a dialogue with the procurator Festus, arguing with him in private about 'justice, self-control and future judgment' until Festus grew alarmed and terminated the conversation (24:25). In summary, then, we may say that Paul included some degree of dialogue in most if not all his preaching, to Christians and non-Christians, to Jews and Gentiles, to crowds and individuals, on formal and informal occasions. Indeed, to add a final text, Paul seems to have expected all the disciples of Jesus to be involved in continuous dialogue with the world, for he urged the Colossians: 'Let your speech always be gracious, seasoned with salt, so that you may know how you ought to answer every one' (Colossians 4:6). Here are Christians in such close contact with 'outsiders' (v5) that they are able both to speak to them (with gracious and salty speech) and to answer their questions.

The kind of 'dialogue' which was included in Paul's ministry was, however, very different from what is often meant by the word today. For Paul's dialogue was clearly a part of his proclamation and subordinate to his proclamation. Moreover, the subject of his dialogue with the world was one which he always chose himself, namely Jesus Christ, and its object was always conversion to Jesus Christ. If this was still the position, few who hesitate about dialogue would disagree with it. But often the modern dialogue of Christians with non-Christians seems to savour rather of unbelief, than of faith, of compromise than of proclamation. It is time now to investigate this argument against dialogue. Afterwards I will seek to marshal some arguments in favour of true dialogue. Then I shall conclude with some contemporary examples.

THE ARGUMENT AGAINST DIALOGUE

The conservative Christian's argument against dialogue

as bordering on treason against Jesus Christ can best be understood historically. The World Missionary Conference at Edinburgh in 1910 took place in an atmosphere of great confidence. I do not call it 'self-confidence,' because certainly their confidence was in God. Nevertheless, they confidently predicted the imminent collapse of the non-Christian religions. Temple Gairdner in his official account of the conference could write: 'The spectacle of the advance of the Christian Church along many lines of action to the conquest of the five great religions of the modern world is one of singular interest and grandeur' (*Edinburgh, 1910*). This mood was rudely shaken by the outbreak of the first World War four years later. And at the second missionary conference at Jerusalem in 1928, the atmosphere was already different. Delegates were aware of the growth of secularism, and even suggested that against this universal enemy a common religious front was necessary.

Ten years later, in 1938, the third ecumenical missionary conference was held at Tambaram near Madras. Its key figure was the Dutchman Henrik Kraemer, whose book *The Christian Message in a non-Christian World* had been written and published shortly before the conference assembled. Partly under the influence of Karl Barth's dialectic, in which he opposed religion to revelation as man's religiosity over against God's word, Kraemer stressed that there was a fundamental 'discontinuity' between the religions of man and the revelation of God. He rejected both aggressive Christian missions on the one hand and on the other the notion that Christ was the fulfilment of non-Christian religions (popularized by J. N. Farquhar's *The Crown of Hinduism*, OUP, 1913), and in their place he urged the uncompromising announcement of the gospel, although 'in a persuasive and winning manner.' He called the church to repossess its faith 'in all its uniqueness and adequacy and power,' and added: 'We are bold enough to call men out from these (*sc.* other religions) to the feet of Christ. We do so because we believe that in him alone is the full salvation which man needs' (quoted by James A. Scherer in his contribution to *Protestant Cross-Currents in Mission*, Abingdon, 1968).

As the Tambaram Conference closed, the black storm clouds of the second World War, and of the new paganism it threatened to unleash, were already darkening the horizon, and when the war ended and ecumenical activity began again, 'the coming dialogue between east and west' which Kraemer had foretold was already being canvassed by other voices. Both Protestant and Roman Catholic theologians began to formulate very differently from Hendrik Kraemer the relation between Christianity and other religions. In 1963 H. R. Schlette could write that 'anyone who determines his ethical and actual individual way of life on the basis of an authentic desire to live a human life according to an order founded on truth, attains salvation' (quoted by Carl F. Hallencreutz in *New Approaches to Men of Other Faiths*, wcc, 1969). Similarly, Karl Rahner in his *Theological Investigations V* (Darton, Longman and Todd), began to popularize the idea that the sincere non-Christian should rather be thought of as an 'anonymous Christian': 'Christianity does not simply confront the member of an extra-Christian religion as a mere non-Christian but as someone who can and must already be regarded in this or that respect as an anonymous Christian.' In consequence, 'the proclamation of the gospel does not simply turn someone absolutely abandoned by God and Christ into a Christian, but turns an anonymous Christian into someone who also knows about his Christian belief in the depths of his grace-endowed being by objective reflection and by the profession of faith . . .' It is in line with this thinking that Raymond Pannikar has written his book, *The Unknown Christ of Hinduism* (Darton, Longman and Todd) and that Professor John Macquarrie has urged the replacement of competitive missions (adherents of different religions trying to convert each other) with a common mission undertaken by all the great religions together 'to the loveless and unloved masses of humanity.'

One of the fundamental beliefs of ecumenical scholars who think and write like this today is that Christ is already present everywhere, including other religions. This being so, it is in their view presumptuous of the Christian missionary to talk of 'bringing' Christ with him into a situation; what he does is first to 'find' Christ already there and then maybe to 'unveil' him. Some go further still. They not only deny that missionaries take Christ with them, or can be the media of Christ's self-revelation to the non-Christian; they even suggest that it is the non-Christian who is the bearer of Christ's message to the Christian. For example, during the discussions on dialogue in Section II at Uppsala, one of the World Council's secretariat proposed the following wording: 'In this dialogue Christ speaks through the brother, correcting our limited and distorted understanding of the truth.' If this wording had been agreed, not only would the non-Christian have been acclaimed as 'the brother,' but the only reference to Christ speaking in the dialogue would have been of his speech to the Christian through the non-Christian. This would have turned evangelism upside down and presented dialogue as the proclamation of the gospel to the Christian by the non-Christian! Fortunately, as a result of pressure from evangelical Christians, the wording was changed to read: 'Christ speaks in this dialogue, revealing himself to those who do not know him and correcting the limited and distorted knowledge of those who do.' I do not think we should object to this formulation.

But is Christ present in the non-Christian world? In our increasingly pluralistic society and syncretistic age, this is the basic theological question which we cannot dodge. It would be facile to reply with a bare 'yes' or 'no.' We need rather to ask ourselves what Christ's apostles taught on this crucial issue. We will look in turn at statements of Peter, Paul and John.

Peter began his sermon to Cornelius: 'Truly I perceive that God shows no partiality, but in every nation any one who fears him and does what is right is acceptable to him' (Acts 10:34, 35). Some have argued from this assertion that sincere religious and righteous people are saved, especially because the story begins with an angel's statement to Cornelius that 'your prayers and your alms have ascended as a memorial before God' (v4). But such a deduction is inadmissible. To declare that a man who fears God and practises righteousness is 'acceptable' to him cannot mean that he is 'accepted' in the sense of being 'justified.' The rest of the story makes this plain. This sincere, godfearing and righteous man still needed to hear the gospel. Indeed, when Peter later recounted to the Jerusalem church what had happened, he specifically recorded the divine promise to Cornelius about Peter, namely that 'he will declare to you a message by which you will be saved' (Acts 11:14). And the Jerusalem church reacted to Peter's account by saying: 'then to the Gentiles also God has granted repentance unto life' (11:18). It is clear then that, although in some sense 'acceptable' to God, Cornelius before his conversion had neither 'salvation' nor 'life.'

In his two sermons to heathen audiences, in Lystra and in Athens, the apostle Paul spoke of God's providential activity in the pagan world. Although in the past God had allowed all the nations 'to walk in their own ways,' he said, yet even then 'he did not leave himself without witness, for he 'did good' to all people, especially by giving them rain, fruitful seasons, food and happiness (Acts 14:16, 17).

To the Athenian philosophers Paul added that God the Creator was the sustainer of our life ('since he himself gives to all men life and breath and everything') and the lord of history ('having determined allotted periods and the boundaries' of all men's 'habitation') intending that men 'should seek God in the hope that they might feel after him and find him.' For 'he is not far from each one of us' since, as heathen poets had said, 'in him we live and move and have our being' and 'we are indeed his offspring.' What these truths and the Athenians' knowledge of them did, however, was not to enable them to find God but rather to make their idolatry inexcusable. For, having overlooked it in the past, God 'now ... commands all men everywhere to repent' (Acts 17:22–31).

This sketch Paul filled out in the early chapters of Romans. He affirms there very clearly the universal knowledge of God and of goodness in the heathen world. On the one hand God's 'invisible nature, namely his eternal power and deity' are 'clearly perceived in the things that have been made,' God having 'shown it to them'

(Romans 1:19, 20). On the other hand, men know something of God's moral law, for he had not only written it on stone tablets at Sinai; he had written it also on men's hearts, in the moral nature they have by creation (2:14, 15). So to some degree, Paul says, all men know God (1:21), know God's law and 'know God's decree' that lawbreakers 'deserve to die' (1:32). This revelation of God to all men, called 'general' because made to all men and 'natural' because given in nature and in human nature, is not, however, enough to save them. It is enough only to condemn them as being 'without excuse' (1:20; 2:1; 3:19). For the whole thrust of the early chapters of Romans is that, although men know God, they do not honour him as God but by their wickedness suppress the truth they know (1:18, 21, 25, 28).

We turn now to John, and especially the prologue to the Fourth Gospel. Here he describes Jesus as 'the Logos of God,' and 'the light of men' (John 1:1–3). He also affirms that the light is continually shining in the darkness and that the darkness has not overcome it (v5). Next he applies these great axioms to the historical process of revelation. He says of the Logos whom he later identifies as Jesus Christ: 'The true light that enlightens every man was coming into the world.' Indeed, 'he was in the world' all the time (vv9, 10). Long before he actually 'came' into the world (v11) he 'was' already in it and was continuously 'coming' into it. Moreover, his presence in the world was (and still is) an enlightening presence. He is the real light, of which all other lights are but types and shadows, and as the light he 'enlightens every man.' Thus 'every man,' Scripture gives us warrant to affirm, possesses some degree of light by his reason and conscience. And we should not hesitate to claim that everything good, beautiful and true, in all history and in all the earth, has come from Jesus Christ, even though men are ignorant of its origin. At the same time we must add that this universal light is not saving light. For one thing it is but a twilight in comparison with the fulness of light granted to those who follow Jesus as 'the light of the world' and to whom is given 'the light of life' (John 8:12). For another thing, men have always 'loved darkness rather than light because their deeds were evil.' Because of their wilful rejection of the light men are under condemnation (John 3:18–21).

The witness then of Peter, Paul and John is uniform. All three declare the constant activity of God in the non-Christian world. God has not left himself without witness. He reveals himself in nature. He is not far from any man. He gives light to every man. But man rejects the knowledge he has, prefers darkness to light and does not acknowledge the God he knows. His knowledge does not save him; it condemns him for his disobedience. Even his religiosity is a subtle escape from the God he is afraid and ashamed to meet.

THE PLACE OF ELENCTICS

We do not therefore deny that there are elements of truth in non-Christian systems, vestiges of the general revelation of God in nature. What we do vehemently deny is that these are sufficient for salvation and (more vehemently still) that Christian faith and non-Christian faiths are alternative and equally valid roads to God. Although there is an important place for 'dialogue' with men of other faiths (as I shall shortly argue), there is also a need for 'encounter' with them, and even for 'confrontation,' in which we seek both to disclose the inadequacies and falsities of non-Christian religion and to demonstrate the adequacy and truth, absoluteness and finality of the Lord Jesus Christ.

This work is technically called 'elenctics,' from the Greek verb *elengchein*, to 'convince,' 'convict' or rebuke,' and so to call to repentance. J. H. Bavinck devotes the whole of Part II of his book, *An Introduction to the Science of Missions* (Hodder and Stoughton, 1954) to this subject, and describes the nature, place, task and main lines of elenctics. He defines it as 'the science which unmasks to heathendom all false religions as sin against God, and . . . calls heathendom to a knowledge of the only true God.' So important does he consider this science to be that it ought, he urges, 'to have a respected position within the context of a theological faculty.' For a full understanding of his thesis I must refer the reader to the fifty pages in which he carefully elaborates it. I wish only to draw attention now to a few of his main points.

First, the purpose of elenctics is not to 'show the absurdity of heathendom,' still less to ridicule other religions or their adherents. It refers chiefly 'to the conviction and unmasking of sin, and to the call to responsibility.' 'In all elenctics the concern is always with the all-important question: "what have you done with God?"'

Next, the justification for this task is the Bible itself, for 'the Bible from the first page to the last is a tremendous plea against heathenism, against the paganizing tendencies in Israel itself, in short, against the corruption of religion.' The Bible also teaches us 'concerning the human heart and its sly attempts to seek God and at the same time to escape him.'

Thirdly, elenctics is not the harsh or negative activity it may sound. It 'can actually be exercised only in living contact with the adherents of other religions.' So 'in practice I am never concerned with Buddhism, but with a living person and *his* Buddhism, I am never in contact with Islam but with a Moslem and *his* Mohammedanism.' Further, this living contact must also be a loving contact.

As long as I laugh at his foolish superstition, I look down upon him; I have not yet found the key to his soul. As soon as I understand that what he does in a noticeably naïve and childish manner, I also do and continue to do again and again, although in a different form; as soon as I actually stand next to him, I can in the name of Christ stand in opposition to him and convince him of sin, as Christ did with me and still does each day.

A fourth and final point is that ultimately elenctics is the work of the Holy Spirit. It is he who 'convicts' of sin, righteousness and judgment (John 16:8–10). 'He alone can call to repentance and we are only means in his hand.'

The very concept of 'elenctics' is out of accord with the diffident, tolerant mood of today. But no Christian who accepts the biblical view of the evil of idolatry on the one hand and of the finality of Jesus Christ on the other can escape it. Further, only those who see the need for elenctics can also see the need for dialogue and can understand its proper place. Only when we are assured that a true

Christian dialogue with a non-Christian is not a sign of syncretism but is fully consistent with our belief in the finality of Jesus Christ, are we ready to consider the arguments by which it may be commended. They are four.

THE ARGUMENT FOR DIALOGUE

First, true dialogue is a mark of *authenticity*. Let me quote the Uppsala statement:

> A Christian's dialogue with another implies neither a denial of the uniqueness of Christ, nor any loss of his own commitment to Christ, but rather that a genuinely Christian approach to others must be human, personal, relevant and humble. In dialogue we share our common humanity, its dignity and fallenness, and express our common concern for that humanity.
>
> *Report II, para. 6*

If we do nothing but proclaim the gospel to people from a distance, our personal authenticity is bound to be suspect. Who are we? Those listening to us do not know. For we are playing a role (that of the preacher) and for all they know may be wearing a mask. Besides, we are so far away from them, they cannot even see us properly. But when we sit down alongside them like Philip in the Ethiopian's chariot, or encounter them face to face, a personal relationship is established. Our defences come down. We begin to be seen and known for what we are. It is recognized that we too are human beings, equally sinful, equally needy, equally dependent on the grace of which we speak. And as the conversation develops, not only do we become known by the other, but we come to know him. He is a human being too, with sins and pains and frustrations and convictions. We come to respect his convictions, to feel with him in his pain. We still want to share the good news with him, for we care about it deeply, but we also care now about him with whom we want to share it. As the Mexico report put it, 'true dialogue with a man of another faith, requires a concern both for the Gospel and for the other man. Without the first, dialogue becomes a pleasant conversation. Without the second, it becomes irrelevant, unconvincing or arrogant' (*Witness in Six Continents*, 1964). Dialogue puts evangelism into an authentically human context.

Secondly, true dialogue is a mark of *humility*. I do not mean by this that proclamation is always arrogant, for true proclamation is a setting forth of Jesus Christ as Saviour and Lord, and not in any sense or degree a parading of ourselves. What I mean rather is that as we listen to another person, our respect for him as a human being made in God's image grows. The distance between us diminishes as we recall that if he is fallen and sinful, so are we. Further, we realize that we cannot sweep away all his cherished convictions with a brash, unfeeling dismissal. We have to recognize humbly that some of his misconceptions may be our fault, or at least that his continuing rejection of Christ may be in reality a rejection of the caricature of Christ which he has seen in us or in our fellow Christians. As we listen to him, we may have many such uncomfortable lessons to learn. Our attitude to him changes. There may after all have been some lingering sense of superiority of which we were previously unconscious. But now no longer have we any desire to score points or win a victory. We love him too much to boost our ego at his expense. Humility in evangelism is a beautiful grace.

Thirdly, true dialogue is a mark of *integrity*. For in the conversation we listen to our friend's real beliefs and problems, and divest our minds of the false images we may have harboured. And we are determined also ourselves to be real. Bishop Stephen Neill distinguishes between dialogue and an 'amiable discussion.' In an article about Bangkok published in *The Churchman* in December 1973 he wrote:

Anyone brought up in the Platonic tradition of dialogue knows well the intense seriousness involved; Socrates and his interlocutors are concerned about one thing only—that the truth should emerge. This is the concern of the Christian partner in dialogue. If Christ is the Truth, then the only thing that matters is that Christ should emerge, but Christ as the Truth makes categorical demands on the individual for total, unconditional and exclusive commitment to himself. It may well be that I may discover in dialogue how inadequate my own self-commitment is; but, out of respect for the freedom and dignity of the partner,

I may not hope and ask for him anything less than I ask and hope for myself. As experience shows, it is extremely difficult to find in any of the non-Christian religions and anti-religions a partner who is prepared to engage in dialogue on this level of seriousness.

Yet such integrity is essential to true dialogue.

Fourthly, true dialogue is a mark of *sensitivity*. Christian evangelism falls into disrepute when it degenerates into stereotypes. It is impossible to evangelize by fixed formulae. To force a conversation along predetermined lines in order to reach a predetermined destination is to show oneself grievously lacking in sensitivity both to the actual needs of our friend and to the guidance of the Holy Spirit. Such insensitivity is therefore a failure in both faith and love. Dialogue, however, to quote from Canon Max Warren 'is in its very essence an attempt at mutual "listening," listening in order to understand. Understanding is its reward' (from an unpublished paper entitled *Presence and Proclamation*, read at a European Consultation on Mission Studies in April 1968). It is this point which was picked up in the Lausanne Covenant, which contains two references to dialogue. On the one hand it says firmly that we 'reject as derogatory to Christ and the gospel every kind of syncretism and dialogue which implies that Christ speaks equally through all religions and ideologies' (para. 3). But on the other it says with equal firmness that 'that kind of dialogue whose purpose is to listen sensitively in order to understand' is actually 'indispensable to evangelism' (para. 4). The principle was stated centuries ago in the Book of Proverbs: 'If one gives answer before he hears, it is his folly and shame' (Proverbs 18:13).

In conclusion, having looked at some of the arguments against and for the place of dialogue in evangelism, I would like to give examples of it in three different contexts, the first among Hindus in India, the second among Moslems in the Arab world, and the third in the industrial areas of Britain.

DIALOGUE WITH HINDUS

My first example is E. Stanley Jones, the American Methodist missionary in India, who flourished between

the wars. He was a prolific writer. His two best-known
books, in which he described the principles of his work,
are probably *The Christ of the Indian Road* (Abingdon Press,
1925) and *Christ at the Round Table* (Hodder and
Stoughton, 1928).

It was during one of his missions that a Hindu invited
him to a tea-party in his home in order that he might meet
some of the leading Hindus of the local community. They
sat in a circle on the floor and talked. Stanley Jones asked
them what their reaction would be if Christ were to come
to India direct, disassociated from Westernism. The
mayor of the city interrupted: 'I hear you speak about
finding Christ. What do you mean by it?' In reply Stanley
Jones told the story of his conversion. 'Now tell me,' said
the mayor, 'how *I* could find him' (*Round Table*). Out of
that conversation Stanley Jones' famous 'Round Table
Conferences' grew. He would invite about fifteen adherents of other faiths—mostly educated people like judges,
government officials, doctors, lawyers and religious
leaders—and five or six Christians, mostly Indians.

In the dialogue which developed, the emphasis was
neither on the rival civilizations of East and West, nor on
the rival Scriptures of Hindus and Christians, nor even on
the rival personalities of Krishna and Christ, but on what
each man's religion meant to him in his own experience.
This has been criticized for example by Hendrik
Kraemer, and we cannot help agreeing that human
testimony does seem rather to have eclipsed the divine
objective testimony to Christ in Scripture. Nevertheless,
God honoured it. Once a Hindu who had written a
savage assault on Christianity, using the latest ammuni-
tion supplied by the Rationalistic Association of Britain of
which he was a member, was challenged to speak at a
deeper personal level and was immediately disconcerted
and silenced. Then a Christian youth with bare feet and
wearing simple homespun spoke naturally of what the
Lord Jesus meant to him. 'There were milleniums of spiritual and social culture between the rest of the group and
this youth,' wrote Stanley Jones, but no one could gainsay
the reality, the authenticity with which he spoke (*Round
Table*).

Two particular aspects of Stanley Jones' 'Round Table' method impress me. The first is his insistence on fairness and mutual respect. Much Western writing about Hinduism had been very polemical, and had unjustly concentrated on the caste system and on idolatry, child widows and the abuses of temple Hinduism rather than on the philosophic thought of the Upanishads and the Bhagavad Gita. 'I felt I would be unfair,' wrote Stanley Jones, 'if I did not let these representatives speak and interpret their own faith . . . Each was given the chance to say the best he could about his own faith.' At the beginning of each conference Stanley Jones would say: 'Let everyone be perfectly free, for we are a family circle; we want each one to feel at home, and we will listen with reverence and respect to what each man has to share.' As a result, the old 'battle of wits' gave place to an atmosphere of 'deep seriousness.'

We have tried to understand sympathetically the viewpoint of the other man.

The deepest things of religion need a sympathetic atmosphere. In an atmosphere of debate and controversy the deepest things, and hence the real things of religion, wither and die.

The Crusaders conquered Jerusalem and found in the end that Christ was not there. They had lost him through the very spirit and methods by which they sought to serve him. Many more modern and more refined crusaders end in that same barrenness of victory.

Yet this does not mean that Stanley Jones was indifferent to the results of his Round Table Conferences, for he was an evangelist. The second impressive point about his conferences is that in them all the supremacy of Jesus Christ was apparent.

There was not a single situation that I can remember where before the close of the Round Table Conference Christ was not in moral and spiritual command of the situation.

At the end everything else had been pushed to the edges as irrelevant and Christ controlled the situation.

No-one could sit through these Conferences and not feel that Christ was Master of every situation, not by loud assertion, or through the pleading of clever advocates, but by what he is and does.

At the close of one conference a Hindu said: 'Today eight of us have spoken and none of us has found; five of you Christians have spoken and all of you seem to have found. This is very extraordinary.' During another conference a Hindu lawyer got up, took the flowers from the table, walked across the room, laid them at the feet of a Christian, touched his feet and said: 'You have found God. You are my guru.'

DIALOGUE WITH MOSLEMS

My second example concerns not the Hindu but the Moslem world. There has been an honorable succession of scholarly and dedicated Christian missionaries to Moslems. One has only to mention the names of Henry Martyn, Samuel Zwemer and Temple Gairdner to realize what great men of God have given their minds and their lives to the task of communicating Christ to the followers of Mohammed. In our own generation one of the best-known names in this field is Bishop Kenneth Cragg, whose dialogical approach to Moslems seems to have been the main inspiration of the series of 'Christian Presence' books which Canon Max Warren has edited. Kenneth Cragg's full statement appears in his book *The Call of the Minaret* (Lutterworth, 1956). He interprets the Muezzin's call not only as an explicit summons to prayer addressed to Moslems, but also implicitly as a call to Christians to respond to the challenge of the Moslem world. So his book is divided into two main parts, the first entitled 'Minaret and Muslim,' in which he expounds the essentials of Muslim belief, and the second 'Minaret and Christian,' in which he issues his fivefold call to us—a call to understanding, to service, to retrieval (the attempt to retrieve the situation in which Moslems are so deeply suspicious of Christians), to interpretation and to patience.

In reading the book two particular emphases have struck me. The first is Bishop Cragg's stress on what he calls 'the ambition for understanding.' If we want to be understood, we must first ourselves struggle to understand. And the kind of understanding he envisages is not merely the academic knowledge which may be gained by a study of Islamics but the far more intimate awareness which comes from the fullest meeting with Muslims. It is from people not just from books that we shall come to understand. The Christian 'must strive to enter into the daily existence of the Muslims, as believers, adherents and men.'

To begin with, the Christian must understand what Islam means to the Moslem. We must 'seek to know it, as far as may be, from within. We wish to hear at the minaret what it is which greets every rising sun and salutes every declining day for millions of contemporary men, and thus to enter with them across the threshold of the mosque into their world of meaning.'

But next the Christian must also understand how Christianity looks to the Moslem. The Christian must feel the shame of the Crusades and of the bitter Medieval polemic against Islam, and grasp the Muslim's abhorrence of Western imperialism and secularism, and his utter non-comprehension of the West's unjust espousal of Israel at the Arabs' expense. The Christian must also strive to understand what Bishop Cragg calls the Muslim's 'massive misunderstandings' of Christian theology—of the Christian doctrines of God and the Trinity, of Christ and the cross, and of salvation.

But the minaret's call to the Christian is not to understanding only. It is also, secondly, to action, and that both negatively and positively. Bishop Cragg uses the word 'retrieval' to indicate the work of restitution which we Christians have to perform. 'Among the factors contributing to the rise of Islam,' he writes, 'was the Christian failure of the Church. It was a failure in love, in purity, and in fervour, a failure of the spirit . . . Islam developed in an environment of imperfect Christianity,' even of a 'delinquent Christianity.' So the Christian

. . . yearns to undo the alienation and to make amends for the past by as full a restitution as he can achieve of the Christ to Whom Islam is a stranger. The objective is not, as the Crusaders believed, the repossession of what Christendom has lost, but the restoration to Muslims of the Christ Whom they have missed.

Let it be clear that the retrieval is not territorial . . . The retrieval is spiritual. It aims not to have the map more Christian but Christ more widely known . . . The retrieval does not mean

taking back cathedrals from mosques, but giving back the
Christ. . . . To restore Christ transcends all else.

Already Bishop Cragg's concept of 'retrieval' has
become positive. It leads naturally to his next call, which
is for interpretation.

If Christ is what Christ is, He must be uttered. If Islam is what
Islam is, that 'must' is irresistible. Wherever there is misconcep-
tion, witness must penetrate: wherever there is obscuring of the
beauty of the cross it must be unveiled: wherever men have
missed God in Christ He must be brought to them again.

We present Christ for the sole, sufficient reason that He
deserves to be presented.

So Bishop Cragg gives himself to the work of interpretation, and in so doing traverses five major theological
areas—the Scriptures, the person of Jesus, the cross, the
doctrine of God, and the Church. Throughout he pleads
for patience, for 'patience with monumental misunderstandings which must somehow be removed,' indeed for
'that travail in patience which is the Christian mission.'

Bishop Stephen Neill writes similarly moving words in
his chapter on Islam in his *Christian Faith and Other Faiths*
(OUP, 1961):

Christians must persist in their earnest invitation to true
dialogue; they must exercise endless patience and refuse to be
discouraged. And the burden of all their invitation must be
'Consider Jesus' . . . We have no other message . . . It is not the
case that the Muslim has seen Jesus of Nazareth and has rejected
him; he has never seen him, and the veil of misunderstanding
and prejudice is still over his face . . .

DIALOGUE IN INDUSTRIAL BRITAIN

My third example of Christian dialogue brings us to post-
Christian Britain, and to the concern of Bishop David
Sheppard for the unreached industrial masses of our own
country. It is well known that after his Islington curacy he
served for eleven years as Warden of the Mayflower
Family Centre in Canning Town, before becoming Bishop
of Woolwich in 1969 and now Bishop of Liverpool. My
quotations are from his book *Built as a City* (Hodder and
Stoughton) published in 1974. His overriding concern is
that

. . . the Church's life in big cities has been marked by its inability to establish a strong, locally rooted Christian presence among the groups that society leaves without voice or power.

Great efforts have been made over the years by many churches in urban and industrial areas . . . But in spite of it all locally rooted churches with strong local leadership are rarely to be seen.

Consequently urban mission 'is not a marginal subject for Christians' but rather 'one of the priorities today in God's work.' 'The gap between Church and world, and especially the world of industry and manual work, is historically wide and contemporaneously massive.' What if anything can be done?

Being the modest man he is, David Sheppard tells no dramatic success story. But he lays down certain basic indigenous principles: 'The Church which will make Jesus Christ and His claims a serious adult proposition will need to have at least four characteristics: a Church of and for the area; a believing and worshipping Church; a common life providing unjudging and thought-provoking fellowship, and local leaders and decision-makers.' Then after the principles he gives some illustrations of how an indigenous working class church can emerge. He writes first of the need for 'bridge-building.' Christians have to care enough to give priority in their time 'to join together with other people in the community,' and together to identify and then to tackle some of the important social issues of their own locality.

From bridge-building he moves to friendship. He tells us that in 1960 he and his wife Grace made a decision: 'we set aside every Thursday evening as a couple to meet couples who did not come to church but with whom we had good links.' On alternate Thursdays they visited couples in their homes and entertained couples in their own home.

We said in the invitation that there was a discussion at the end of the evening. In our flat there was always background music, for a visit to a vicar's home is a nerve-racking adventure for non-church people, and sitting on the edge of chairs in silence is to be avoided. A cup of tea, gossip, sometimes a noisy game called Pit, another cup of tea and some sandwiches and half an hour's discussion. On evenings like these after some had gone home, and in visits to homes, a high proportion of the best conversations started at 10.30 p.m.

From bridge-building through friendship expressed in informal evenings of relaxed discussion they moved to a more serious 'searching-group.' 'Five couples came. They already had the self-confidence that they would not be thought foolish whatever ideas they expressed. I learned then just how powerful a learning weapon has been created when a "talking-group" has come into being, whose members sense that the others feel the same way about life.' After two and a half years, David Sheppard could write, 'a number of local couples were convinced Christians.' Canon David Edwards, reviewing the book in the *Church Times* (25 January 1974) commented: 'His book is pre-eminently a call to patience in real life and real love. He summons us to keep on keeping on.'

I hope and believe that these three examples, although from very different contexts—Hindu, Moslem and post-Christian—all illustrate the same marks of a true Christian dialogue, which I have called authenticity, humility, integrity and sensitivity. Dialogue is a token of genuine Christian love, because it indicates our steadfast resolve to rid our minds of the prejudices and caricatures which we may entertain about other people; to struggle to listen through their ears and look through their eyes so as to grasp what prevents them from hearing the gospel and seeing Christ; to sympathize with them in all their doubts, fears and 'hang-ups.' No one has expressed this better than Lord Ramsey of Canterbury in his little critique of secular theology called *Images Old and New* (SPCK, 1963). He insists upon our duty to 'go out and put ourselves with loving sympathy inside the doubts of the doubting, the questions of the questioners, and the loneliness of those who have lost the way.' For such sympathy will involve listening, and listening means dialogue. It is once more the challenge of the Incarnation, to renounce evangelism by inflexible slogans, and instead to involve ourselves sensitively in the real dilemmas of men.

4 Salvation

'Mission' denotes what God sends his people into the world to do, and of primary importance within this mission of sacrificial service is 'evangelism,' the sharing with others of God's good news about Jesus. 'Dialogue,' a serious conversation in which we listen as well as speak, is an activity closely related to evangelism. On the one hand it is an activity in its own right, whose goal is mutual understanding. On the other, since the Christian is under the constraint of love to bear witness to Christ, dialogue is also a necessary preliminary to evangelism. Indeed it is the truly human and Christian context within which his evangelistic witness should be given. To confess this frankly does not destroy the integrity of the dialogue on the ground that it now has an ulterior motive, and has degenerated into an exercise in public relations whose real objective is the conversion of the other man. This candour rather preserves the integrity of the dialogue by preserving the integrity of the Christian who participates in the dialogue. For the Christian would be true neither to himself nor to his partner in the dialogue if he concealed either his belief in the universal lordship of Jesus or his longing that his partner will join him in submission to Jesus as Lord. Such submission in penitence and faith is the way of 'salvation,' which is the fourth word we are to consider. What does 'salvation' mean?

THE CENTRALITY OF SALVATION
Let the word drop into the middle of a conversation with the unsuspecting, and it is sure to provoke either a blush or a smile or a frown. For some people find salvation language embarrassing or funny, while others assert that it

is a meaningless inheritance from the traditional religious vocabulary of the past. Certainly, then, if Christians are to continue to use the word, it needs to be translated into a more modern idiom. This is fine, even essential, on condition that we remain loyal to the biblical revelation. For a translation is one thing (the old message in new words); a fresh composition is something quite different. The integrity of a translator lies in his resolve to subordinate his rendering to the intention of the original author. Privately he may disagree with the author but he has no liberty to correct him. Translation is not a synonym for manipulation.

Perhaps I should entitle this chapter 'salvation yesterday and today,' for what concerns me is whether attempted modern reconstructions are really what biblical authors were writing about. The Third Assembly of the Commission on World Mission and Evangelism, which took place in Bangkok from 9 to 12 January 1973, was immediately preceded by a World Conference entitled *Salvation Today*. It is this which prompts the question whether the Bangkok interpretation of 'Salvation Today' is true to the understanding of salvation yesterday, namely to the teaching of Jesus and his apostles about what 'salvation' is.

It may be good at once to recognize how vital this question is. For it is no exaggeration to say that Christianity is a religion of salvation. The God of the Bible is a God who has kept coming to the rescue of his people, who has taken the initiative to save. Six times in the Pastorals he is called 'God our Saviour.' ' "God" and "Saviour" are synonymous throughout the whole of the Old Testament,' writes Michael Green (*The Meaning of Salvation*, Hodder and Stoughton, 1965). The same could be said about the New Testament for the mission of Jesus was a rescue mission. He 'came into the world to save sinners' (1 Timothy 1:15). 'The Father has sent his Son as the Saviour of the world' (1 John 4:14). His very name embodies his mission, for 'Jesus' means 'God the Saviour' or 'God is salvation' (Matthew 1:21), and his full title is 'our Lord and Saviour Jesus Christ' (*eg* 2 Peter 3:18).

Hence the Bible is a *Heilsgeschichte*, a history of God's

mighty saving acts. Indeed, it is more than a chronicle of the past; it is a contemporary handbook of salvation, 'able to instruct you for salvation through faith in Christ Jesus' (2 Timothy 3:15). And of course the gospel is called 'the good news of your salvation' (Ephesians 1:13), even 'the power of God for salvation to every one who has faith' (Romans 1:16), because it is through the *kerygma* that God chooses to 'save those who believe' (1 Corinthians 1:21). This prominence of the salvation theme in biblical Christianity obliges us to ask what it is which God works, which Christ achieves, which Scripture unfolds and which the gospel offers. I have to begin with two negatives.

SALVATION AND PHYSICAL HEALTH
First, salvation does not mean psycho-physical health.

It became a fashion soon after the second World War to equate salvation with health, and especially with 'wholeness' understood as a kind of composite health embracing body, mind and spirit. One of the chief proponents of this view has been Miss Phyllis Garlick who delivered the 1943 James Long lectures at Oxford under the title *The Wholeness of Man* (Highway Press). She later developed her thesis in her book on the inter-relation of religion and medicine entitled *Man's Search for Health*, which was published by Highway Press in 1952.

Her emphasis is that physical and mental healing 'is of the very essence of the gospel of the grace of God.' She never goes quite so far as to say that healing equals salvation, but she gets very near it. 'The saving power of the grace of God is for the whole man.' Again '"to seek and to save" . . . implies a conception of healing which does not stop short at cure and relief for the sufferer, but has for its aim a restored, renewed, invigorated personality,' Her final chapter is called 'Wholeness: "an idea whose time has come."' In it she gives her understanding of Christ's purpose in terms of 'life' rather than of 'salvation.' 'Christ came not to preserve life but to develop it to the full; to make man every whit whole.' Miss Evelyn Frost in her earlier book *Christian Healing* (1940) actually referred to physical health as an aspect of eternal life now. She wrote

of 'the great Christian truth that there is eternal life for
the whole of man.' Again, 'Christian healing for body and
mind as well as for spirit is an integral part of the
Christian gospel.'

These concepts were given further expression in the booklet *The Healing Church*, published in Geneva in 1965, a
report of an ecumenical conversation in Tübingen the
previous year. A trenchant criticism of it appeared in 1970
put out by the Christian Medical Fellowship of London,
namely *The Healing Church: an Ambiguous and Misleading
Concept* by Dr Stanley G. Browne, the renowned
leprologist.

Let me try to clarify the point at which I am venturing
to criticize Miss Frost and Miss Garlick. I am not denying
that according to Scripture, disease is an alien intrusion
into God's good world, nor that it is often ascribed to the
malevolent activity of Satan, nor that God heals both
through natural means and sometimes supernaturally (for
all healing is divine healing), nor that Jesus's miraculous
healings were signs of his kingdom, nor that he showed
both indignation towards sickness and compassion towards the sick, nor that illness, pain and death will find no
place in the new bodies and the new universe which God
is going one day to create. For I believe and hope that
these truths are common ground. I would go further and
say that a greater measure of health often follows an experience of salvation. Now that psychosomatic medicine
attributes many conditions to stress, while social medicine
attributes others to environmental causes, it is to be expected that salvation, because it often leads to the relief of
stress and to an improved environment, will also
sometimes bring healing of mind and body. Moreover, all
Christians should be able to affirm joyfully with Paul that
the life of Jesus can be manifested in our mortal flesh (2
Corinthians 4:10, 11) and that the power of Jesus is made
perfect in our human weakness (2 Corinthians 12:9, 10 *cf*
4:7). For our new life in Christ can often bring a new
sense of physical and emotional well being. What I do
deny is that this healing, or indeed any kind of healing—
natural or supernatural—either is, or is included in, what
the Bible means by the salvation which is now offered to

mankind by Christ through the gospel.

Of course at the consummation, God will redeem the total creation including our human bodies, and this may rightly be termed full and final salvation, but to assert that healing is as readily and as instantly available today as salvation, or that such healing is part of the salvation which God offers us in Christ by faith now, or that believing Christians have no business ever to be ill, is an attempt to anticipate the resurrection and redemption of our bodies. Not till then will disease and death be no more.

Some modern radical theologians have tried to reinterpret salvation in terms of psychological rather than physical health. Take as an example, Bishop John Robinson in *Honest to God* (SCM, 1965). Having dispensed with a transcendent personal God and replaced him with 'the ground of our being,' he asks what 'reconciliation' can mean when there is no God to be reconciled to. In answer he seizes on the phrase in the Parable of the Prodigal Son that 'he came to himself' and proposes that, since God is the ground of our own being, salvation is coming to ourselves. Salvation becomes a kind of psychological integration, the wholeness of a balanced personality. Without doubt many disintegrated personalities do find a new integration through reconciliation with God. But we must not identify reconciliation with integration. Further, there is no hermeneutical justification for asserting that 'he came to himself' equals 'he came to his father,' for in the parable of Jesus these were not the same thing but two distinct and consecutive stages in the prodigal's restoration.

One result of the confusion of salvation and health is that the roles of the doctor and the parson also become confused. Either the practitioner replaces the pastor, or the pastor transforms himself into an amateur psychiatrist. In his perceptive booklet *Will Hospital Replace the Church?* (Christian Medical Fellowship, 1969), Dr Martyn Lloyd-Jones, who himself gave up being a consultant physician in order to become a pastor, agrees that the hospital has quite rightly taken over the healing of the sick. Then he adds: 'The Hospital does not, cannot, and never will be able to take over the functions of the Church! It is quite impossible for it to do so ... The authentic task of the

Church is not primarily to make people healthy . . . her
essential task is to restore men to right relationship with
God . . . Man's real problem is not simply that he is sick,
but that he is a rebel.'

At this stage in my argument some may wish to reply
that the word 'salvation' *is* used in the New Testament,
particularly in the gospels, to denote a physical deliverance. They are quite right—at least verbally—and we
need to examine their point. *Sōzō* is used of deliverance
from blindness (in the case of blind Bartimaeus, Mark
10:52), from leprosy (Luke 17:19) and from an issue of
blood (Mark 5:34). In each case Jesus said to the sufferer
'your faith has saved you,' which each time the
Authorized Version renders 'thy faith hath made thee
whole.' The same was said of a crowd of people who were
sick with unspecified diseases. As many as touched
Christ's garment, we are told, 'were made well,' which in
the Greek is *esōzonto*, 'were saved' and in the Authorized
Version, 'were made whole' (Mark 6:56, *cf* Acts 14:9,
James 5:15). But *sōzō* is also used of deliverance from
drowning ('Save, Lord, we are perishing' Matthew 8:25 *cf*
14:30 and Acts 27:20, 31, 34 and 43–28:4) and even from
death ('Save yourself, and come down from the cross! . . .
He saved others; he cannot save himself' Mark 15:30, 31 *cf*
John 12:27, Hebrews 5:7).

All this is true. But what does it prove? Are we to argue
from these uses of the verb 'to save' that wherever the
New Testament promises salvation to the believer it is
offering him not only deliverance from sin but also a kind
of comprehensive insurance against physical ills of every
kind, including disease, drowning and even death? No. It
would be impossible to reconstruct the biblical doctrine of
salvation in these terms. Salvation by faith in Christ
crucified and risen is moral not material, a rescue from sin
not from harm, and the reason why Jesus said 'your faith
has saved you' to both categories is that his works of
physical rescue (from disease, drowning and death) were
intentional signs of his salvation, and were thus understood by the early church.

We need to remember that the miracles of Jesus were
constantly called *sēmeia*, signs of his kingdom, signs of his

salvation. Further, the apostles recognized them to be such, and no doubt used these miracle-stories in their preaching and teaching. Jesus's well-known words 'your faith has saved you' were spoken to the fallen woman who anointed his feet and whom he forgave (Luke 7:48–50). They were also spoken to the blind man, the leprosy sufferer and the woman with the issue of blood not because their cure was their salvation, but because it was a dramatized parable of it.

The form-critical interpretation of the gospels strongly suggests such an evangelistic use of these well-known incidents. For example, sin is a chronic inward moral disease, which no human being can cure, and if we turn to human remedies we shall not improve but rather get worse. So let the sinner put out the hand of faith and let him but touch the hem of Christ's garment, and he will be made whole, that is, saved. Again, do the storms of sinful passion and even of the wrath of God threaten to engulf us? Then let us cry to Jesus Christ, 'Save, Lord, we are perishing,' and immediately he will still the storm, we shall not perish but be saved, and go on to enjoy the peace and calm of his salvation. This is how the early church used these stories of physical deliverance. They believed Jesus had intended them to be illustrations of salvation, not promises of safety or health.

Similarly, the apostle Peter after healing the congenital cripple outside the temple gate could move straight from the means by which 'this man has been saved' (*sesōstai*, RSV 'has been healed') to the affirmation that 'There is salvation (*sōtēria*) in no one else, for there is no other name under heaven given among men by which we must be saved (*sōthēnai*) (Acts 4:9, 12). The man's healing was 'a notable sign' (4:16) of his salvation.

SALVATION AND POLITICAL LIBERATION

I come now to my second negative, that salvation is not socio-political liberation.

The second major attempted reconstruction of the doctrine of salvation locates man's chief predicament not in his physical and mental sicknesses, but in his social and political structures. It therefore reinterprets salvation as the liberation of deprived and disadvantaged people from hunger, poverty and war, from colonial domination, political tyranny, racial discrimination and economic exploitation, from the ghettos, the political prisons and the soulless technology of the modern world. Not disease but oppression is the problem; so salvation is justice, not health. The most striking recent example of this formulation comes from the ecumenical Assembly at Bangkok in January 1973 already mentioned, but it may be helpful to trace some of the steps which led to it.

When the International Missionary Council was merged with the World Council of Churches at New Delhi in 1961 the aim of the Commission on World Mission and Evangelism was defined as 'to further the proclamation to the whole world of the gospel of Jesus Christ to the end that all men may believe in him and be saved,' while its functions were said to include prayer and exhortation so that the churches would complete 'the unfinished evangelistic task' and forward 'the spread of the gospel in the world.' It is clear from these expressions that the salvation in view at that time was a personal deliverance from sin by faith as a result of the proclamation of the gospel.

Two years later, in December 1963, CWME had its first full meeting in Mexico City. It asked the question: 'What is the form and content of the salvation which Christ offers men in the secular world?' (*Witness in Six Continents*), but it acknowledged its inability to give a satisfactory answer. Then in 1968 the two reports on 'the missionary structure of the congregation' were published together, the one from Western Europe entitled *The Church for Others*, and the other from North America entitled *The Church for the World*. These reports were formative of the thinking expressed in Section II of the Uppsala Assembly later the same year. In them 'the goal of mission' was defined as 'humanization.' Christ was said to be 'the true man, the head of the new humanity,' and so 'wherever men and women are led to restored relationships in love of neighbour, in service and suffering for the sake of greater justice and freedom,' these things must be recognized as 'signs of the fulness of humanity' which Christ is providing (*The Church for Others*). The *Drafts for Sections* published in preparation for Uppsala quoted extensively from these two reports, and borrowed from them the notion that the goal of mission may be defined equally well in terms either of 'the new humanity' or of the establishment of '*shalom*' (peace seen as 'a social happening, an event in inter-personal relations') or of the kingdom of God. In answer to Mexico City's question about the relation between God's action through the Church and God's action in the world apart from the Church, they came down heavily on the latter, and on the Church's duty 'to make the world's agenda our business.' Much of this thinking was reflected in the final report of Section II at Uppsala, although it was somewhat toned down during the process of composition.

Another document which was influential at Uppsala was the report of the *Conference on Church and Society* which had been held in Geneva in 1966, with its emphasis on the theme of world development. An ecumenical *Consultation on Development* at Montreux took place in 1970, and a preparatory paper by a member of the CWME staff on the theology of mission and development included the statement, 'God's salvation of mankind in Christ encompasses the development of all of men's faith, institutions and structures . . . True development is the battle for the wholeness of man both individual and corporate' (*From Mexico City to Bangkok*). The return to the concept of man's 'wholeness' is significant, conceived now more in socio-political than in psycho-physical terms.

During the five years between Uppsala (1968) and Bangkok (1973) the ecumenical emphasis shifted from humanization and development to the secular liberation movements, and the 'Programme to Combat Racism' (launched in 1969) gathered momentum. As at Uppsala so at Bangkok no reconciliation of disputed points was reached, and the Assembly's Report contains mutually exclusive positions. It is stated that 'salvation is Jesus Christ's liberation of individuals from sin and all its consequences' (Bangkok Assembly *1973*) and that 'our concentration upon the social, economic and political implications of the gospel does not in any way deny the personal and eternal dimensions of salvation.' Yet this is the impression which the Report as a whole creates.

In the section on 'salvation and social justice in a divided humanity' come these assertions: 'The salvation which Christ brought, and in which we participate, offers a comprehensive wholeness in this divided life . . . It is salvation of the soul and the body, of the individual and society, mankind and "the groaning creation" (Romans 8:19) . . . As guilt is both individual and corporate, so God's liberating power changes both persons and structures . . . Therefore we see the struggles for economic justice, political freedom and cultural renewal as elements in the total liberation of the world through the mission of God.' Thus salvation is liberation, and liberation changes people and structures equally. Not only is this equation itself a very dubious one (as we shall see), but the report then goes on to delineate 'salvation in four dimensions— economic, political, social and personal—and even affirms that in one sense 'salvation is the peace of the people in Vietnam, independence in Angola, justice and reconciliation in Northern Ireland and release from the captivity of power in the North Atlantic community' just as much as it is 'personal conversion in the release of a submerged society into hope' or 'new life styles amidst corporate self-interest and lovelessness.'

This brief historical sketch of ecumenical thinking during the 10 years from Mexico 1963 to Bangkok 1973 has shown that the emphasis has been on key words like 'humanization,' 'development,' 'wholeness,' 'liberation' and 'justice.' Let me say at once that these things, and the liberation of men from every form of oppression, are not only a desirable goal, pleasing to God the Creator, but that Christians should be actively involved in pursuing it alongside other men of compassion and goodwill. For God created all men and cares for all men. He means human beings to live together in peace, freedom, dignity and justice. These things in every society are the concern of God, for the God of the Bible is a God of justice as well as of justification and he hates injustice and tyranny. Further, we evangelicals have often been guilty of opting out

of our social and political responsibilities. We are to blame
for this neglect. We should repent of it and not be afraid
to challenge ourselves and each other that God may be
calling many more Christians than hear his call to im-
merse themselves in the secular world of politics, econ-
omics, sociology, race relations, community health,
development and a host of other such spheres for Christ.

THE THEOLOGY OF LIBERATION
Not long before Bangkok the original Spanish version of
Gustavo Gutierrez's book, *A Theology of Liberation* was
published in Peru. This was in 1971, although the English
translation did not appear in America until 1973 or in
Britain (scm) until 1974. Subtitled *History, Politics and
Salvation*, this is the fullest and most thorough attempt
which has yet been made to interpret biblical salvation in
terms of the liberation of the oppressed.

The 'theology of liberation' is an authentic product of
Latin America. Beginning with historical reality rather
than with Scripture or tradition, and drawing on the help
of the social sciences, it registers its spirited protest against
the theologies of North America and Europe. Its best
known exponents apart from Gustavo Gutierrez are
Ruben Alves (*Theology of Human Hope*) and Hugo
Assmann (*Oppression–Liberation: A Challenge to Christians*).
Professor Orlando Costas distinguishes them by saying
that 'if Alves is the prophet of the movement, and Assman
is the apologist, then Gutierrez is the systematic
theologian' (*The Church and Its Mission: A Shattering Critique
from the Third World*, Coverdale, 1974).

The background to Gutierrez's book is threefold: Latin
America the 'oppressed continent,' the Roman Catholic
church and its *aggiornamento*, and Marxist economic
theory. I admire the deep compassion of Gustavo
Gutierrez for the exploited, his insistence on solidarity
with the poor, his emphasis on social 'praxis' instead of
unpractical theorizing, and his call to the church for 'a
more evangelical, more authentic, more concrete and
more efficacious commitment to liberation.' Several
times he quotes with approval Marx's famous dictum
that 'the philosophers have only *interpreted* the

world . . .; the point, however, is to *change* it.'

We should have no quarrel with the goal he defines, namely 'liberation from all that limits or keeps man from self-fulfilment, liberation from all impediments to the exercise of his freedom.' This is fully biblical. God made man in his own image; we should oppose all that dehumanizes him. Again, 'the goal is not only better living conditions, a radical change of structures, a social revolution; it is much more: the continuous creation, never ending, of a new way to be a man, a *permanent cultural revolution.*'

What are the means to this end? One of the recurrent themes of the book is that history is the process in which man grows in self-consciousness, 'gradually takes hold of the reins of his own destiny,' wins his freedom, and thus creates a new society. In sociological and technological terms man has indeed 'come of age.' He now possesses in full measure that 'dominion' which God told him to exercise at the beginning of creation (Genesis 1:26–28).

All this—the need for man to free and to fulfil himself, and to take responsibility for the restructuring of his society—is biblical and right. Both the end and the means are well defined. It is when the author begins to theologize, to try to present social liberation as if this were what Scripture means by salvation, and so to dispense with evangelism in favour of political action, that— reluctantly but decidedly—I part company with him.

He himself asks the basic question: 'What relation is there between salvation and the historical process of the liberation of man?' It is, he adds, 'the classic question of the relation between . . . faith and political action, or in other words between the Kingdom of God and the building up of the world.' He hangs back from identifying the two. But he comes very close to it, and in order to do so indulges in some extremely dubious exegesis.

He all but obliterates the distinction between church and world, Christian and non-Christian, in order that he may apply to all men the biblical teaching about God's saving work. Whether they are conscious of it or not, he writes, 'all men are in Christ efficaciously called to communion with God.' Indeed this, he dares to add, is 'the

Pauline theme of the universal lordship of Christ, in whom all things exist and have been saved.' It also 'gives religious value in a completely new way to the action of man in history, Christian and non-Christian alike. The building of a just society has worth in terms of the Kingdom, or in more current phraseology, to participate in the process of liberation is already in a certain sense a salvific work.'

In the chapter entitled 'Encountering God in history,' he again universalizes the work and the presence of God. Beginning with the 'temple' imagery of Scripture he goes on to make the statement, entirely unwarranted even on his own premises, that 'the Spirit sent by the Father and the Son to carry the work of salvation to its fulfilment dwells in every man.' Again, 'since God became man, humanity, every man, history is the living temple of God.' And Christ's 'liberation creates a new chosen people, which this time includes all humanity.' There is absolutely no biblical justification for such statements. On the contrary, the New Testament authors constantly contradict this notion by insisting on the distinction between those who are in Christ and those who are not, those who have the Spirit and those who have not (*eg* Romans 8:9; 1 John 5:12).

Is there no place, then, in Gutierrez's scheme for conversion? Yes, but it is fundamentally 'conversion to the neighbour.' He has already affirmed that 'man is saved if he opens himself to God and to others, even if he is not clearly aware that he is doing so.' The struggle to be unselfish and 'to create an authentic brotherhood among men' is itself a response to God's grace, whether the people concerned explicitly confess Christ as Lord or not. Indeed, the only way to love God is to love my neighbour, the only way to know God is to do justice. Now certainly a true love and knowledge of God must issue in love and justice to our neighbour, but to put this the other way round and make the knowledge of God the consequence of doing justice, and even to equate the two, is uncommonly like a doctrine of salvation by good works.

The author keeps urging that beyond and through 'the struggle against misery, injustice and exploitation the goal

is the *creation of a new man.*' He knows that this is both a
Marxist and also a biblical expression. But he betrays no
embarrassment that although the words are the same, the
sense in which they are used may be different. The 'one
new man' or 'single new humanity' of which Paul writes is
God's creation by Christ's death and God's gift to those
who are personally in Christ (Ephesians 2:15, 16; 2 Corinthians 5:17). It is hard to believe that Dr Gutierrez
seriously thinks this is the same as the 'creation' through
Marxism of a new social order and life style for all men
whether Christian or not.

THE HERMENEUTICAL QUESTION

Although liberation from oppression and the creation of a
new and better society are definitely God's good will for
man, yet it is necessary to add that these things do not
constitute the 'salvation' which God is offering the world
in and through Jesus Christ. They could be included in
'the mission of God,' as we have seen, in so far as
Christians are giving themselves to serve in these fields.
But to call socio-political liberation 'salvation' and to call
social activism 'evangelism'—this is to be guilty of a gross
theological confusion. It is to mix what Scripture keeps
distinct—God the Creator and God the Redeemer, the
God of the cosmos and the God of the covenant, the world
and the church, common grace and saving grace, justice
and justification, the reformation of society and the regeneration of men. For the salvation offered in the gospel
of Christ concerns persons rather than structures. It is
deliverance from another kind of yoke than political and
economic oppression.

Perhaps at no time was this confusion more evident
at Bangkok than when analogies were drawn between
Chairman Mao and Jesus Christ. One of the documents
published in preparation for the conference was entitled
Salvation Today and Contemporary Experience. On one page
somebody claims to have been 'saved by Mao,' while on
the next someone else claims to have been saved by Jesus
Christ. Similarly an American delegate said: 'Chairman
Mao is God's Messiah to the Chinese,' and a large poster
appeared one day on the conference notice-board which,

after a reference to the West's 'compulsive neurosis' to convert China, said 'Salvation? God save China from conversion!' Now it may well be possible to say that Mao has 'saved' China in the sense of giving it a new national identity. But one could only say this by overlooking the appalling loss of human life and liberty by which such a national 'salvation' has been obtained. And it is childish to the point of blasphemy to equate this kind of 'salvation' with the saving work of our Lord Jesus Christ.

One's deep uneasness about current ecumenical writing is basically hermeneutical. It concerns the treatment of Scripture, both Old Testament and New Testament, with which its proponents attempt to buttress it. Several critics of Bangkok have alluded to the misuse of Scripture at ecumenical assemblies. It is sometimes arbitrarily selective (omitting what is inconvenient), and at other times extremely cavalier (twisting what seems convenient in order to support a preconceived theory).

Father Jerome Haber, an American Roman Catholic from the Vatican Secretariat, was invited to evaluate the Bangkok conference as it concluded. He spoke in French, but has been translated as follows: 'I am appalled that you people can discuss "Salvation Today" day after day . . . but not listen to what the Apostle Paul said about it. I haven't heard anyone speak on justification by faith. I've heard no one speak of everlasting life' (quoted by Arthur Glasser in *The Evangelical Response to Bangkok*, William Carey Library, 1973).

Similarly, Bishop Stephen Neill has written: 'The salvation which is conceived in purely three-dimensional terms ends by being no salvation at all. Perhaps the gravest weakness of this Assembly is that its title was wrongly chosen; there is hardly anything about salvation in any New Testament sense of the term in its pages and proceedings' (*The Churchman*, December 1973).

The main biblical evidence adduced for the Bangkok position was drawn from the Old Testament, namely the liberation of Israel from their Egyptian oppressors. Gustavo Gutierrez leans heavily on the same interpretation of the Exodus. The people of Israel were slaves. 'The starting point is oppression in the form of economic exploitation and by means of a policy of population control' (*Biblical Perspectives on Salvation*). In their bondage they 'groaned' and cried to God, and God told Moses he knew their oppression and had 'come down to deliver (or liberate) them' (Exodus 3:7–10). Years later at the Red Sea they were told to 'stand firm and see the salvation of the Lord.' When the rescue was complete, it was written 'thus the Lord saved Israel,' and Israel became known as 'the people whom God had redeemed' (Exodus 14:13; 14:30; 15:13). The pre-Bangkok comment on this biblical teaching asks the crucial questions whether it can be applied 'to each group of oppressed people' and whether it can be regarded as 'the type of liberation which God intends for all the downtrodden.' It leaves these questions unanswered. But surely the answer must be 'no.'

Certainly oppression in every form is hateful to God. Certainly too God is active in the history of every nation. So much so that his word through Amos drew an analogy between Israel on the one hand and the Philistines and Syrians on the other: 'Did I not bring up Israel from the land of Egypt, and the Philistines from Caphtor and the Syrians from Kir?' (Amos 9:7). But this was to assert that Israel could not monopolize Yahweh as if he were a tribal deity; it did not deny the special relationship which God had established between himself and his people Israel. On the contrary, it was again through Amos that God asserted the uniqueness—and therefore the moral implication—of this relationship: 'You only have I known of all the families of the earth; therefore I will punish you for all your iniquities' (Amos 3:2 *cf* Psalm 147:20). It was this same special relationship which lay behind the Exodus. God rescued his people from Egypt in fulfilment of his covenant with Abraham, Isaac and Jacob and in anticipation of its renewal at Mount Sinai (Exodus 2:24; 19:4–6). He made no covenant with the Syrians or the Philistines, nor did his providential activity in their national life make them his covenant people. In Scripture, 'salvation' and 'covenant' always belong together. Hence in the New Testament the Exodus becomes a picture of ation for all politically oppressed minorities.

We can have no objection to the use of the word 'salvation' in a political sense, provided it is clear that we are not talking theologically about God's salvation in and through Christ. For example, there is no need to quarrel with Alexander Solzhenitsyn that in his famous 'Letter to the Soviet Leaders' (dated 5 September 1973 and published in the West in March 1974) he sets out what he holds to be 'for the good and salvation of our people.' But when the New Testament handles Old Testament promises of salvation, it interprets them in moral rather than material terms. Perhaps the most striking example is the *Benedictus* in which the 'horn of salvation' which God had raised up, according to his promise through the prophets 'that we should be saved from our enemies,' is understood in terms of serving God 'in holiness and righteousness,' while John the Baptist will 'go before the Lord to prepare his ways, to give knowledge of salvation to his people in the forgiveness of their sins' (Luke 1:67–79).

Another popular biblical passage used at Bangkok was our Lord's quotation from Isaiah in the Nazareth synagogue: 'The Spirit of the Lord is upon me, because he has anointed me to preach good news to the poor. He has sent me to proclaim release to the captives and recovering of sight to the blind, to set at liberty those who are oppressed . . .' (Luke 4:18). Here three main categories of people are mentioned—the poor, the captives and the blind—and it was assumed at Bangkok that literal, physical conditions are envisaged. But can we take this so easily for granted? It is true that during his ministry Jesus opened the eyes of the blind, and certainly the blind should arouse our Christian compassion today. But Christ's miraculous restoration of sight was a sign that he was the light of the world; it can hardly be taken as an instruction to us to perform similar miraculous cures today. Jesus also ministered to the poor and had some disconcerting things to say to the rich. Yet it is well known that 'the poor' in the Old Testament were not just the needy but the pious whose hope and trust were in God. The first Beatitude cannot possibly be understood as making material poverty a condition of receiving God's kingdom, unless we are prepared to turn the gospel upside down.

What then of captives and the oppressed? There is no evidence that Jesus literally emptied the prisons of Palestine. On the contrary the main prisoner we hear about (John the Baptist) was left in prison and was executed. What Jesus did do, however, was to deliver people from the spiritual bondage of sin and Satan, and to promise that the truth would set his disciples free.

Please do not misunderstand me. Material poverty, physical blindness and unjust imprisonment are all conditions which in different degrees dehumanize human beings. They should provoke our Christian concern and stimulate us to action for the relief of those who suffer in these ways. My point, however, is that deliverance from these things is not the salvation which Christ died and rose to secure for men.

I have one further exegetical point to make regarding the attempt to interpret salvation in terms of social liberation. It concerns the instructions which the apostles give to slaves in the New Testament. Although they do not directly attack the institution of slavery, yet Paul insists that slaves are to be treated 'justly and fairly' (Colossians 4:1). This was a revolutionary assertion, for the concept of 'justice' for slaves was never contemplated in the Roman Empire. Indeed, it is this demand for justice which undermined the institution and in the end destroyed it. Further, although Paul does not incite slaves to rebellion, civil disobedience or self-liberation, yet he does encourage them, if they can gain their freedom, to avail themselves of the opportunity. He thus recognizes that slavery is an offence to human dignity. 'Do not become slaves of men,' he writes. But then he adds these significant words: 'he who was called in the Lord as a slave is a freedman of the Lord . . . So, brethren in whatever state each was called, there let him remain with God' (1 Corinthians 7:20–24). The importance of this teaching should be clear. Slaves who can gain their social freedom should do so, for this is God's will for them. But if they cannot, let them remember that in Christ, whatever their social condition, they are still free men! Their slavery cannot inhibit their deepest liberty as human beings who have been set free by Jesus Christ, nor can it destroy their dignity as those whom God has accepted. They can stay even in their slavery 'with God.' No doubt I am laying myself open to the old charge of religious drug peddling, of yet more 'opium for the people.' But such an accusation would not be fair. It would never be legitimate to use those two words 'with God' to condone oppression or to justify an uncritical acquiescence in the status quo. At the same time, they can transform every situation. For they tell us that Jesus Christ gives an inward freedom of the spirit which even the most oppressive tyrant cannot destroy. Think of Paul in prison: was he not free?

So far I have been largely negative. I have tried to argue from Scripture that the 'salvation' which Christ once died to win and now offers to men is neither psycho-physical healing nor socio-political liberation. In rejecting these attempted reconstructions I have also tried to guard myself against misunderstanding. It is necessary to balance my negatives with three positive assertions. First, God is greatly concerned for both these areas, namely our bodies and our society. Secondly, one day both body and society will be redeemed. We shall be given new bodies and shall live in a new society. Thirdly, love compels us meanwhile to labour in both spheres, seeking to promote physical health (by therapeutic and preventive means) and seeking to create a radically different social order which will bring men freedom, dignity, justice and peace. Nevertheless, having emphasized the importance of these things to God and therefore to us, we still have to affirm that they are not the salvation which God is offering human beings in Christ now.

The Lausanne Covenant expresses the tension clearly: 'We affirm that God is both the Creator and the Judge of all men. We therefore should share his concern for justice and reconciliation throughout human society and for the liberation of men from every kind of oppression. Because mankind is made in the image of God, every person, regardless of race, religion, colour, culture, class, sex or age, has an intrinsic dignity because of which he should be respected and served, not exploited . . . Although reconciliation with man is not reconciliation with God, nor is social action evangelism, nor is political liberation salvation, nevertheless we affirm that evangelism and socio-political involvement are both part of our Christian duty. For both are necessary expressions of our doctrines of God and man, our love for our neighbour and our obedience to Jesus Christ. The message of salvation implies also a message of judgment upon every form of alienation, oppression and discrimination, and we should not be afraid to denounce evil and injustice wherever they exist . . .' (para. 5).

SALVATION AND PERSONAL FREEDOM

What is salvation, then? It is personal freedom. True, it sometimes results in increased physical and mental health, as we have seen, True also it has far-reaching social consequences for, as the Lausanne Covenant puts it, 'the salvation we claim should be transforming us in the totality of our personal and social responsibilities' (para. 5). Nevertheless, salvation itself, the salvation Christ gives to his people, is freedom from sin in all its ugly manifestations and liberation into a new life of service, until finally we attain 'the glorious liberty of the children of God.' Werner Foerster and Georg Fohrer in their combined article in Kittel's *Theological Dictionary* are agreed that salvation words are primarily negative and emphasize what we are saved from. Thus in the Greek world, salvation was first and foremost 'an acutely dynamic act in which gods or men snatch others by force from serious peril,' whether perils of battle and of the sea, of judicial condemnation or illness. Hence in Greek literature, doctors, philosophers, judges, generals, rulers and specially the emperor are numbered among human 'saviours.'

The commonest salvation verb in the Old Testament has the basic idea of broadness or roominess as opposed to the narrowness of some oppression. It thus indicated deliverance out of some imprisonment into spaciousness 'through the saving intervention of a third party in favour of the oppressed and in opposition to the oppressor.' 'The thought,' Georg Fohrer continues, 'is neither that of self-help nor of co-operation with the oppressed. The help is such that the oppressed would be lost without it.' It may be a city which is rescued from a besieging army, a nation from a foreign régime, the poor from injustice, or individuals from some personal calamity.

All this is an important background for our understanding of the salvation of *God*. He is the living God, the Saviour; idols are dead and cannot save. And when God saves his people, he not only rescues them from the oppressor but he saves them for himself. 'You have seen what I did to the Egyptians,' he said 'and how I bore you on eagles' wings and brought you to myself' (Exodus 19:4). This is the theme already mentioned that 'salvation' and 'covenant' belong together. Similarly the 'new song' of praise to Christ in heaven declares: 'thou wast slain and by thy blood didst ransom men for God . . .' (Revelation 5:9).

Now freedom is as popular a word today as salvation is unpopular. But unfortunately most contemporary talk about freedom is negative. Dictionaries define it negatively. One says it is 'the absence of hindrance, restraint, confinement, repression.' Another says that to be free is to be 'not enslaved, not imprisoned, unrestricted, unrestrained, unhampered.' And the dictionaries are only reflecting common usage. But we must never define freedom in purely negative terms. Indeed the insistence on a positive understanding of freedom is a distinctively Christian contribution to current debate. Lord Ramsey has written: 'We know what we want to free men *from*. Do we know what we want to free men *for*?' He goes on to insist that our striving for those freedoms 'which most palpably stir our feelings' (*ie* freedom from persecution, arbitrary imprisonment, racial discrimination, crippling hunger and poverty) should always be 'in the context of the more radical and revolutionary issue of the freeing of man from self and for the glory of God.' Such freedom, he continues, is seen perfectly in Jesus alone: 'He is free from someone and free for someone. He is free from self, and free for God' (*Freedom, Faith and the Future*, SPCK).

So we shall now examine the New Testament doctrine of salvation, in its familiar three phases or tenses, and in each case observe how the negative and positive aspects complement each other. 'Liberation' is a good rendering of 'salvation,' not least because it hints at the liberty into which the liberated are brought.

FREEDOM FROM JUDGMENT FOR SONSHIP

In its past phase, 'salvation' is liberation from the just judgment of God upon sin. It is not just that we had guilt feelings and a guilty conscience, and found relief from these in Jesus Christ. It is that we were actually and objectively guilty before God and have now received a free remission of our guilt, which caused the bad feelings and bad conscience. The reason why the gospel is 'the power of God for salvation' is that in it 'the righteousness of God is revealed' (namely his righteous way of declaring the unrighteous righteous), and the reason for this revelation of the righteousness of God in the gospel is the revelation of 'the wrath of God . . . from heaven against all ungodliness and wickedness of men who by their wickedness suppress the truth.' This logical sequence of thought in Romans 1:16–18 links the power of God, the righteousness of God and the wrath of God. It is because his wrath is revealed against sin that his righteousness is revealed in the gospel and his power through the gospel to believers.

In this past phase, 'salvation' is the equivalent of 'justification,' which itself is the opposite of condemnation. All those who are 'in Christ' are *sesōsmenoi* (Ephesians 2:8, 9), those who have been saved, as they are *dikaiōthentes* (Romans 5:1), those who have been justified. Indeed, Romans 10:10 specifically equates the two, for 'man believes with his heart and so is *justified*, and he confesses with his lips and so is *saved*.' This justification has been made possible only because of the propitiatory sacrifice of Christ (Romans 3:24–26). There is 'no condemnation for those who are in Christ Jesus' only because God sent his own Son 'in the likeness of sinful flesh and as a sin offering' and 'condemned sin in the flesh,' that is, in the flesh in which Jesus came (Romans 8:1–3). Of course the wrath of God is not like human wrath, nor is the propitiation of Christ like heathen propitiations. But once all unworthy elements have been eliminated, namely the concept of the arbitrary wrath of a vengeful deity being placated by the paltry offerings of men, we are left with the Christian propitiation in which God's own love sent his own dear Son to appease his own holy wrath against sin (1 John 2:2; 4:10).

In their unfolding of the first phase of salvation, however, the apostles go further than the propitiation of God's wrath, and further even than God's justification of the sinner, which is his acceptance of him as righteous in God's sight. Paul emphasizes that we are saved *from* wrath and *for* sonship. God sent his Son not just to redeem us but also to adopt us into his family. Our judge becomes our father, and the Holy Spirit himself enables us to cry to him, 'Abba, Father,' thus bearing witness with our own spirit that we are indeed his children. So then we are no longer slaves, but sons (Romans 8:14–17; Galatians 4:4–7). Now we are free to live as free men.

In his moving book *Knowing God* (Hodder, 1973) Dr J. I. Packer has written: 'Were I asked to focus the New Testament message in three words, my proposal would be *adoption through propitiation*, and I do not expect ever to meet a richer or more pregnant summary of the gospel than that.'

FREEDOM FROM SELF FOR SERVICE

We turn now to the present phase of salvation. For salvation in the New Testament is as much a present process as a gift received in the past. If you ask me if I am saved, and if I think biblically before I answer, I could just as truly reply 'no' as 'yes.' Yes, I have indeed been saved by the sheer grace of God from his wrath and from my guilt and condemnation. But no, I am not yet saved, for sin still dwells within me and my body is not yet redeemed. It is the common tension in the New Testament between the 'now' and the 'not yet.'

It is well known that the verb *sōzō* is sometimes used in the New Testament in the present tense, as well as in the aorist and the perfect. Christians are *hoi sōzomenoi* ('those who are being saved'). This is partly because it is recognized that our salvation has not yet been brought to completion. *Hoi sōzomenoi* ('those who are being saved') are contrasted with *hoi apollumenoi* ('those who are perishing'), for *they* have not yet perished, and *we* have not yet reached heaven (*cf* 1 Corinthians 1:18; 2 Corinthians 2:15; Acts 2:47). Another reason for the present tense is that during the interim between our justification and our glorification comes that process called sanctification, the gradual transformation of the believer by the Spirit of Christ into the image of Christ 'from one degree of glory to another' (2 Corinthians 3:18) until in the end we shall be fully conformed to the image of God's Son (Romans 8:29; *cf* 1 John 3:2).

Moreover, since Jesus Christ into whose image we are being changed is 'the second man' or 'second Adam' (Romans 5 and 1 Corinthians 15), the pioneer of the new humanity, we ourselves who are in Christ are sharers in this new humanity. To become Christian is in a real sense to become human because nothing dehumanizes more than rebellion against God or humanizes more than reconciliation to God and fellowship with God. But to assert joyfully that salvation includes humanization is not at all the same thing as saying that humanization (rescuing men from the dehumanizing process of modern society) equals salvation.

The ecumenical argument seems to run like this: Salvation according to the New Testament makes men human; therefore whatever makes men human is salvation. But this kind of reasoning is as deficient in logic as in theology. One might just as well say: 'Exercise makes men fit, therefore whatever makes you fit is exercise.' Or 'Aspirin relieves pain, therefore whatever relieves pain is aspirin.'

Salvation as a present process is expressed in two surprising apostolic commands. 'Work out your own salvation,' Paul writes, calling on the Philippians to exhibit in practical everyday living the salvation which God is working within them (Philippians 2:12, 13), while the apostle Peter stresses the need of his readers to 'grow up to salvation' (1 Peter 2:2). Since in the previous verse he has told them to put away all malice, deceit, insincerity, envy and slander, it is evident that he regards these things as babyish and that the 'salvation' he wants them to grow up into is again Christlikeness of behaviour.

In this present salvation too we should emphasize the positive. We are being delivered from the bondage of self-centredness into the liberty of service. Jesus spoke of our being the slaves of sin, and there is no slavery worse than imprisonment in oneself. Luther described fallen man as '*homo in se incurvatus*,' 'man curved or bent inwards upon himself.' From this prison Jesus Christ liberates us. He warns us that if we insist on 'saving' ourselves, holding on to our own life in selfishness, we shall lose ourselves. By contrast, only if we are prepared to lose ourselves by giving ourselves away in service to him and to others, shall we ever truly find ourselves (Mark 8:35). It is only when we die that we live, only when we serve that we are free.

This present salvation, this liberation from the shackles of our own self-centredness into the freedom of service, brings more thoroughgoing demands than we are often prepared to recognize. To quote from the Lausanne Covenant again, 'the results of evangelism include obedience to Christ, incorporation into his church and responsible service in the world' (para. 4). Unless we are truly delivered from a slavish conformity to tradition, convention and the bourgeois materialism of secular culture, unless our discipleship is radical enough to make us critical of establishment attitudes and indignant over all forms of oppression, and unless we are now freely and selflessly devoted to Christ, church and society, we can hardly claim to be saved, or even to be in the process of being saved. Salvation and the Kingdom of God are synonymous (*cf* Mark 10:23–27), and in the Kingdom the authority of Jesus is absolute.

It is impossible to grasp the fulness of this present phase of salvation, as depicted in the New Testament, without feeling ashamed of our contemporary Christian failures. We tend so to glory in our past salvation as a free gift already received that we neglect the call to 'grow up to salvation' and to give ourselves whole-heartedly with our fellow believers to the service of God and man. We should not resist the Uppsala statement that the church itself is a priority situation for mission, to which Philip Potter alluded in his report at Bangkok when he said 'the Church which would be the bearer of salvation today needs itself to be saved, liberated from all that is false to the revolutionary, convicting and renewing nature of the Gospel' (*International Review of Mission*, Vol. lxii).

FREEDOM FROM DECAY FOR GLORY

Thirdly, God's salvation, which is both a gift and a continuing process, is also the object of our Christian hope. We were saved in hope of being saved, and the 'hope of salvation' is the helmet which the Christian soldier wears (Romans 8:24; 1 Thessalonians 5:8).

Each day brings this salvation closer, for 'salvation is nearer to us now than when we first believed' (Romans 13:11 *cf* 1 Peter 1:5, 9). We do not, however, cherish the kind of utopic vision which Gustavo Gutierrez describes in his chapter 'Eschatology and Politics.' On the contrary, 'we reject as a proud self-confident dream the notion that man can ever build a Utopia on earth. Our Christian confidence is that God will perfect his Kingdom and we look forward with eager anticipation to that day and to the new heaven and earth in which righteousness will dwell and God will reign for ever' (*Lausanne Covenant*, para. 13).

What will it be, this final salvation? To begin with, it will be a deliverance from the wrath to come (Romans 5:9; 1 Thessalonians 1:10; 5:9). More than that, it will include 'the redemption of our bodies.' For our bodies share with the whole creation a 'bondage to decay' which makes the creation groan as if in labour and makes *us* groan inwardly as well. We long for our new bodies which will be liberated from physical frailty, a fallen nature and mortality and for the new universe (in which there will be no oppression but only righteousness). This prospect the New Testament also depicts in positive rather than merely negative terms. For our inward groaning is a longing for our 'adoption as sons,' when our sonship will be revealed in its fulness. Similarly, the whole creation will not just 'be set free from its bondage to decay' but will 'obtain the glorious liberty of the children of God' (see Romans 8:18–25; 2 Peter 3:13).

I have tried to show that in each phase of personal salvation Scripture lays its emphasis not on our rescue (from wrath, from self, from decay and death) so much as on the freedom which this rescue will bring—freedom to live with God as our Father, freedom to give ourselves to the service of others, and finally the 'freedom of glory' when, rid of all the limitations of our flesh-and-blood existence, we are free to devote ourselves without reserve to God and to each other.

Are we saved? Yes, and 'we rejoice' (Romans 5:2, 3, 11). Are we saved? No, and in this body with the whole creation, 'we groan inwardly' as we wait for the consummation. We rejoice and we groan: this is the paradoxical experience of Christians who have been saved and are being saved, and at the same time are not yet saved.

So the gospel is the good news of salvation, and like Paul we must be able to declare that we are not ashamed of it. For as Michael Green rightly says at the end of his thorough study *The Meaning of Salvation,* 'there is still a hunger for salvation' in today's world. And God's good news is still his power unto salvation to those who believe. He still saves believers through the *kerygma*, the announcement of Jesus Christ.

Finally, we must exhibit what we proclaim. Dr Radhakrishnan, Hindu philosopher and former President of India, is said to have commented to some Christians: 'You claim that Jesus Christ is your Saviour, but you do not appear to be more "saved" than anyone else.' Our message of salvation is bound to fall on deaf ears if we give no evidence of salvation in a changed life and life-style. This applies to nobody more directly than to the preacher of the gospel. 'The most effective preaching,' writes John Poulton in his *A Today Sort of Evangelism* (Lutterworth, 1972), 'comes from those who embody the things they are saying. They *are* their message . . . Christians . . . need to look like what they are talking about. It is *people* who communicate primarily, not words or ideas . . . Authenticity gets across from deep down inside people . . . What communicates now is basically personal authenticity.' And personal Christian authenticity is an authentic experience of salvation.

5 Conversion

'Mission' is the loving service which God sends his people into the world to render. It includes both evangelism and social action, for each is in itself an authentic expression of love and neither needs the other to justify it. Yet because of the appalling lostness of man there is an insistent urgency about our evangelistic task. The nature of 'evangelism' is a faithful proclamation of the good news. 'Dialogue' is its necessary preliminary inasmuch as listening must precede proclaiming, and the 'salvation' which is its goal is personal freedom through Christ, though with unavoidable social implications in anticipation of the eschatological 'freedom of glory' when God makes all things new. Our fifth word is 'conversion.' It denotes the response which the good news demands and without which salvation cannot be received.

THE CONTEMPORARY DISTASTE FOR 'CONVERSION'

Yet 'conversion' is another unpopular word today. Of course in some circles it has always been distasteful. Upper middle-class English snobs, for example, have tended to regard conversion as decidedly necessary for the lower classes who are the province of the Salvation Army, but hardly necessary for respectable pillars of the Church of England establishment like themselves. In High Church circles too it has often been associated with that dreadful phenomenon 'evangelical enthusiasm.' Bishop J. R. H. Moorman of Ripon has written in his *A History of the Church of England* (A. & C. Black, 1953) of

... that remarkable but eccentric Cornish priest' of the mid-nineteenth century called R. S. Hawker of Morwenstow. He regarded himself as neither High nor Broad nor Low in his churchmanship, since his main interests were with the Eastern Church which he believed to be the mother of Cornish Christianity. His little parish (to which he devoted himself for 41 years) was full of smugglers, wreckers and poachers, and his church of activity and colour. For Sunday services he wore cope, alb and scarlet gloves, and on his wedding day 'a claret-coloured clerical coat, a blue fisherman's jersey, wading-boots up to the hips and a pink hat without a brim.

Perhaps it is no surprise to learn that he had no faith in conversion. According to S. Baring-Gould, his biographer, he regarded it as 'a spasm of the ganglions' (Moorman). I do not know for certain where to locate the ganglions, but then I doubt if R. S. Hawker would have known either!

There is a second reason why people have developed a dislike for the notion of conversion. This concerns the impression of arrogant imperialism which some evangelists have sometimes given. If ever our evangelism descends to the level of 'empire-building,' 'scalp-hunting' or 'line-shooting' (because we brag about the dimensions of the fish we catch), then of course we bring the word 'conversion' into disrepute. It is because of what he calls 'the deliberate attempt to engineer conversions' that Professor J. G. Davies can go so far as to write: 'I would be glad if the term conversion could be dropped from the Christian vocabulary' (*Dialogue with the World*, scm, 1967).

To such perverted forms of evangelism, however, it would be better to apply the term 'proselytism,' for evangelism and proselytism are emphatically not identical activities. True, it is difficult to find a satisfactory definition of each, so that Bishop Lesslie Newbigin has written: 'one is inclined to conclude that the only workable distinction is that evangelism is what we do and proselytism is what others do' (*The Finality of Christ*, scm, 1964). The Central Committee of the World Council of Churches threw some light on this question in their statement of 1960 entitled 'Christian Witness, Proselytism and Religious Liberty in the Setting of the wcc': 'Proselytism . . . is the corruption of witness. Witness is corrupted when cajolery, bribery, undue pressure or intimidation is used— subtly or openly—to bring about seeming conversion;

when we put the success of our church before the honour
of Christ; . . . when personal or corporate self-seeking
replaces love for every individual soul for whom we are
concerned. Such corruption of the Christian witness
indicates lack of confidence in the power of the Holy
Spirit, lack of respect for the nature of man and lack of
recognition of the true character of the Gospel' (wcc
Central Committee Minutes, 1960, quoted by Philip Potter in
his address to the Central Committee in Crete, August
1967). As a matter of fact, the Lausanne Covenant
includes a rather similar statement. It is a confession that
we are guilty of 'worldliness' whenever, 'desirous to ensure
a response to the gospel, we have compromised our message, manipulated our hearers through pressure techniques and become unduly preoccupied with statistics or
even dishonest in our use of them' (para. 12).

Over against the use of coercion and the unseemly spirit
of triumphalism one can welcome J. C. Hoekendijk's insistence upon the opposite qualities: 'To evangelise is to sow
and wait in respectful humility and in expectant hope: in
humility because the seed we sow has to die, in hope
because we expect that God will quicken this seed and
give it its proper body' (*The Church Inside Out*, scm, 1967).

If a sense of social superiority and misguided forms of
evangelism are two reasons for a revulsion against 'conversion,' a third is the doctrines of syncretism and universalism. For syncretism declares that no religion has
finality, while universalism declares that no man is lost.
The most plausible form in which these ideas are
presented today is one which appears to magnify the work
of Jesus Christ. For example, one of the working commit-
tees which studied 'the missionary structure of the congregation' at Bossey in 1964 reported: 'The Passion and
Resurrection of Jesus Christ is the Exodus for all men.
Now the whole of mankind is delivered from bondage and
brought into covenant with God. By the raising up of the
New Man, Christ Jesus, every man has been made a
member of the new mankind' (*Planning for Mission*, edited
by Thomas Wieser, Epworth, 1966). We are told that
'there was intensive discussion on this paragraph' and that
various additions were proposed. Nevertheless, there it

stands, an uncompromising statement of universal salvation already accomplished by Jesus Christ. If it were true
that all men are saved, then the only function left to
'evangelism' would be to acquaint the ignorant of this
good news and 'conversion' would cease to indicate a
change of any kind except in a man's awareness of his true
identity. Scripture does not support this view, however. It
is true that God is described as having done something
objective and decisive through the cross. Thus, 'God . . .
through Christ reconciled us to himself' and 'God was in
Christ reconciling the world to himself.' But this does not
mean that all men have actually been reconciled to God.
For now he commits to us the ministry and the message of
reconciliation. And this ministry and message are not to
inform people that they are already reconciled, but rather
to beg people on behalf of Christ: 'Be reconciled to God.'
What validity would such an appeal have if those who
hear it are already reconciled to God but simply do not
know it? We must never expound God's reconciling work
in and through Christ in such a way that it eliminates the
contemporary need for men to be reconciled to God. As
James Denney expressed it: 'It is in virtue of something
already consummated on His cross that Christ is able to
make the appeal to us which He does, and to win the
response in which we receive the reconciliation' (*The
Death of Christ*, Tyndale).

So if we are to be truly biblical in our understanding,
we must hold together two truths, first that God was 'in
Christ' reconciling the world to himself, and secondly that
we ourselves must be 'in Christ' if we are to receive the
reconciliation (2 Corinthians 5:18–21, *cf* v17, Romans
5:11).

Further, it is our solemn duty to affirm that those to
whom we announce the gospel and address our appeal are
'perishing.' We proclaim to them the good news of Jesus
not because they are saved already but in order that they
may be saved from perishing. Our responsibility is to
'preach peace' in the sense of promising peace with God
through Jesus Christ to those who repent and believe. To
preach peace in the sense of announcing smooth words to
those still in rebellion against God, of saying 'peace, peace

when there is no peace'—this is the word of a false prophet, not of a true evangelist of Jesus Christ. The gospel
brings warning as well as promise, of the retention of sins
as well as the remission of sins (John 20:23). 'Beware,
therefore,' warned the apostle Paul, 'lest there come upon
you what is said in the prophets: "Behold, you scoffers,
and wonder, and perish . . ."' (Acts 13:40, 41). 'Perish' is
a terrible word. So is 'hell.' We may, and I think we
should, preserve a certain reverent and humble agnos-
ticism about the precise nature of hell, as about the
precise nature of heaven. Both are beyond our understanding. But clear and definite we must be that hell
is an awful, eternal reality. It is not dogmatism that
is unbecoming in speaking about the fact of hell; it is
glibness and frivolity. How can we think about hell without tears?

CONVERSION AND REGENERATION

If, then, a response to the gospel is necessary, this response
is called 'conversion.' What does it mean? In the New
Testament the verb *epistrephō* is usually in the middle or
passive voice, and for this reason is six times translated to
'be converted' (*eg* Acts 3:19 AV). But at the same time it
has an active sense and means to 'turn.' When used in
ordinary, secular contexts its first meaning is to 'turn
round' as for example when Jesus turned round in the
crowd to see who had touched him (Mark 5:30). Its other
meaning is to 'return' as when an unwanted greeting
returns to its giver (Matthew 10:13), or the demon determines to return to the house he has vacated (Matthew
12:44), although the more usual verb for returning is *hupo-
strephō*, as when the Bethlehem shepherds returned to their
sheep and the holy family to Nazareth (Luke 2:20, 39).

When the same verb is used theologically, it is evident
that it has not changed its basic meaning. It still signifies
to turn from one direction to another, or to return from
one place to another. Thus, Christians can be described as
having 'turned to God from idols' (1 Thessalonians 1:9 *cf*
Acts 14:15) and also, after 'straying like sheep,' as having
'now returned to the Shepherd and Guardian of your
souls' (1 Peter 2:25). Since the turn from idols and sin is

usually called 'repentance,' and the turn to God and Christ 'faith,' we reach the interesting biblical equation that REPENTANCE + FAITH = CONVERSION.

What, next, is the relation between conversion and regeneration or the new birth? Certainly each belongs to the other as obverse and reverse of the same coin. We can assert without any fear of contradiction that all the converted are regenerate and all the regenerate are converted. It is impossible to envisage or experience either without the other. Nevertheless, they must be distinguished from one another theologically. Three differences may by mentioned.

First, regeneration is God's act, whereas conversion is man's. Regeneration is a new birth, a birth 'from above' (*anōthen*), a birth 'of the Spirit.' It is the peculiar work of the Holy Spirit who himself infuses life into the dead. Conversion, on the other hand, is what we do when we repent and believe. True, both repentance and faith are God's gifts, and we could neither repent nor believe without his grace (*eg* Acts 11:18; 18:27). Nevertheless, what God's grace does is so to set us free from darkness and bondage as to enable us to do the repenting and the believing. I doubt if we need lose sleep over the question which comes first. Scripture seems to accord the priority now to the one, now to the other. The really important truth is that they are inseparable.

Secondly, regeneration is unconscious, whereas conversion is normally conscious. The latter is not always so in the sense that it is a remembered conscious act, for many people brought up in a Christian home have loved God and believed in Jesus from their earliest years and cannot recall a period in which they did not believe or a moment when they first did. To such we must say with Dr Packer that 'convertedness as a condition matters more than conversion as an experience' (in *Evangelicals Today* edited by J. C. King, Lutterworth, 1973). For adults, however, the turn from idols to the living God, and from sin to Christ, is a conscious act of penitence and faith. But regeneration is unconscious. Its results may well be consciously enjoyed, in terms of assurance, release, communion with God, love, joy and peace. Yet the actual passage from death to life is not a felt experience. As John Owen put it in his great (seventeenth century) book *Pneumatologia* or *A Discourse concerning the Holy Spirit*, the regenerating work of the Holy Spirit 'in itself is secret and hidden, and discoverable only by its effects' (footnote 4th Edition 1835, see the whole passage pp76–83 in which he outlines both the differences and the identities in people's experience of the new birth). Indeed, this is what our Lord seems to have meant when he said to Nicodemus: 'the wind blows where it wills, and you hear the sound of it, but you do not know whence it comes or whither it goes; so it is with everyone who is born of the Spirit' (John 3:8). The new birth itself is a mysterious work. Its consequences, however, are plain. An analogy with physical birth may be helpful. We were not conscious of the process of being born; our self-consciousness has developed subsequently. Similarly the reason we may know we are born again is not because we were consciously aware at the time of what was happening, but because we know that our present Christian self-consciousness, or rather God-consciousness, being a mark of spiritual life, must have originated in a spiritual birth.

The third difference between regeneration and conversion is that the former is an instantaneous and complete work of God, whereas the turn of repentance and faith which we call 'conversion' is more a process than an event. There can be no doubt of the suddenness of the new birth. The very imagery of birth makes this clear. For though months of gestation precede it and years of growth follow it, birth itself is a crisis event. We are either born or unborn, just as we are either alive or dead. Further, birth is a complete experience. Once born we can never be more born than at the first moment of emergence from the womb. So with the new birth. To quote John Owen again, regeneration is 'not . . . capable of degrees, so that one should be more regenerate than another. Every one that is born of God is equally so, though one may be more beautiful than another, as having the image of his Heavenly Father more evidently impressed on him, though not more truly. Men may be more or less holy; more or less sanctified; but they cannot be more or less regenerate.'

There is an evident gradualness about many conversions, however. People begin to become troubled in their conscience and to see the need for repentance. The Holy Spirit begins to open their eyes and they begin to see in Jesus Christ the Saviour they need. They may then enter a period of struggle, half resisting, half yielding. They may become like Agrippa 'almost persuaded' or like the epileptic boy's father simultaneously believing and unbelieving. Even Saul of Tarsus, who is supposed to have been history's most conspicuous example of sudden conversion, was really nothing of the kind. We are not to imagine that he had his first contact with Jesus Christ on the Damascus Road, for he had apparently been 'kicking against the goads' of Jesus for some time. Somerset Maugham used a different metaphor to emphasize the variety of 'shapes' under which conversion comes: 'with some men it needs a cataclysm, as a stone may be broken to fragments by the fury of a torrent; but with some it comes gradually, as a stone may be worn away by the ceaseless fall of a drop of water' (*The Moon and Sixpence*, 1919).

No doubt in the experience of many there is a point at which the turn called conversion becomes complete, and dawning faith becomes saving faith. Moreover sometimes people are conscious of this moment. Yet the Holy Spirit is a gentle Spirit; he often takes time to turn people around from self-absorption to Christ. And even then, after we may justly be described as 'converted Christians,' his work is far from done. For although regeneration cannot grow, the repentance and faith which make up conversion may grow, and indeed must. We need a deeper penitence and a stronger faith. Conversion is only a beginning. Before us lies a lifetime of growth into maturity in Christ, of transformation into the image of Christ.

It is sometimes suggested that conversion is a psychological phenomenon common to many religions. William James, for example, in his famous Gifford Lectures, *The Varieties of Religious Experience* (1902), could say: 'Conversion is a process, gradual or sudden, by which a self, hitherto divided and consciously wrong, inferior and unhappy, becomes unified and consciously right, superior and happy, through an establishment of a right relationship with the object of the religious sentiment.' Similarly at Bangkok, Section 1 (*Culture and Identity*) reported: 'Conversion as a phenomenon is not restricted to the Christian community; it finds its place in other religions as well as in certain political and ideological communities' (*Bangkok Assembly*, 1973). If one is thinking merely of a change of allegiance, together with the sense of psychological release which follows a period of tension and struggle, this is so. But Christians will add that there are unique dimensions to the Christian conversion experience, since in it God by his Spirit regenerates the person concerned and 'the object of the religious sentiment' (to borrow William James's expression) is none other than the Lord Jesus Christ.

After this attempt to define conversion, both in itself and in its relation to regeneration, we must now explore certain implications of this radical change.

CONVERSION AND REPENTANCE

First, let us consider conversion and the Lordship of Christ. We saw in the second chapter on evangelism that repentance and faith are the twin demands of the gospel, and we have already noted in this chapter that the two together constitute conversion. It is the element of repentance which is regrettably absent from much modern evangelistic preaching, although it was prominent in the message of our Lord (*eg* Mark 1:15; Luke 13:3, 5) and of his apostles (*eg* Acts 2:38; 3:19; 17:30).

What is needed in preaching repentance today is both integrity and realism. In all our evangelism there must be integrity. Our anxiety to win converts sometimes induces us to mute the call to repentance. But deliberately to conceal this aspect of our message is as dishonest as it is short-sighted. Jesus himself never glossed over the cost of discipleship, but rather summoned would-be disciples to 'sit down first and count the cost,' for he was requiring them if they were to follow him to deny themselves, take up their cross and die. Any kind of slick 'decisionism' which sacrifices honesty on the altar of statistics is bound to cause other casualties as well, the victims of our own folly. We are under obligation to teach that a new life in

Christ will inevitably bring in its wake new attitudes, new ambitions and new standards. For in Christian conversion not only do old things pass away but in their place new things come (2 Corinthians 5:17).

In addition to integrity our preaching of repentance and of Christ's lordship requires realism. It is not enough to call people to repentance in vague terms, as if conversion could take place in a kind of mystical vacuum out of which all real life has been sucked. When John the Baptist preached his baptism of repentance he insisted that people responding must 'bear fruits that befit repentance.' Nor did he leave it there. He went on to specific issues. The affluent must share their surplus wealth with the deprived. Tax collectors must replace extortion by probity. And soldiers must never use their power to rob people, but rather be content with their wages (Luke 3:8, 10–14). Jesus evidently did the same, for Zacchaeus was quite clear that for him discipleship would involve refunding his illicit gains. Then he went on to give half his capital to the poor, presumably because most of the folk he had robbed he would never be able to trace. We too need to spell out in realistic and concrete terms the contemporary implications of repentance, conversion and the lordship of Jesus Christ.

CONVERSION AND CHURCH

The second implication of conversion is church membership. Some influential voices are being raised in our day, however, to the effect that converts should not necessarily be required to join the church. Dr M. M. Thomas in his *Salvation and Humanization* (CLS, Madras, 1971), for example, argued for what he called 'a Christ-centred secular fellowship outside the church' and—in the context of India—'a Christ-centred fellowship of faith and ethics in the Hindu religious community.' He elaborated his position by adding that 'conversion to Christ' should not necessarily imply 'conversion to the Christian community.' Instead converts should seek to build up 'a Christ-centred fellowship of faith within the society, culture and religion in which they live, transforming their structures and values from within.' In his view this might even include a rejection of baptism as having become 'a sign not primarily of incorporation into Christ but of proselytism into a socio-political-religious community.' A convert from Hinduism should not be obliged to separate himself 'from the Hindu community in the social, legal and religious sense.'

Revolutionary as Dr Thomas's proposals sound, I think we need to respond to them sympathetically. The background to his argument is the disastrous development in India and elsewhere of what is usually called 'communalism.' It is the rise of a Christian community which, instead of being scattered throughout the non-Christian community as salt and light, becomes isolated from it as a distinct cultural entity. I shall have more to say about this cultural question later.

A second reason why one can understand M. M. Thomas's position concerns the state of the church which converts are expected to join. As Philip Potter told the Central Committee of the World Council of Churches at its 1967 Crete meeting: 'There is widespread disillusionment with the congregation as it is. Someone engaged in experiments in evangelism in a big city has remarked that "the spiritual poverty and unpreparedness of the Church is such that no one can desire a large number of those now outside to enter the churches as they are."' This is true. I suppose all of us are disenchanted with the ecclesiastical status quo. Yet surely, in the light of this, our Christian duty is to seek the renewal of the church, not to avoid or abandon it. For it still remains God's church, unless of course it has totally apostatized from the revealed truth of God. Even the Corinthian church with its bitter factions, tolerated immorality, disorders of public worship and doctrinal uncertainties was nevertheless addressed by Paul as 'the church of God which is at Corinth' (1 Corinthians 1:2).

Bishop Lesslie Newbigin contributed a sensitive review of Dr M. M. Thomas's book to the March 1971 issue of *Religion and Society*, and posed some searching questions. In later correspondence with Dr Thomas (published in *Asia Focus*, 4th quarter 1972) he described his proposal as quite unrealistic' and added that 'a man who is religiously, culturally and socially part of the Hindu community is a Hindu.'

From this contemporary debate we need to turn back to the Bible and to its consistent witness that through the historical process God has been and still is calling out a people for himself, a people who are to be distinct from the world in their convictions and standards, while remaining immersed in it. According to the Letter to the Ephesians this redeemed community is central both to the gospel and to history. Further, from the Day of Pentecost on, when God's people became the Spirit-filled body of Christ, the apostles expected converts to join it. Peter's summons to the people that very day was not only to repent and believe—as if their conversion could remain an individualistic transaction—but also to be baptized and thus to 'save themselves' from that 'crooked generation' and be 'added' to the new community of the Spirit (Acts 2:40–47). Some kind of transfer from one community to another (I shall later qualify what is meant by 'transfer') was thus envisaged from the beginning.

The necessity for incorporation by baptism into the church was clearly recognized at Bangkok: 'The Christian conversion . . . introduces people into the Christian community . . . Christian conversion gathers people into the worshipping community, the teaching community and the community of service to all men.' Indeed, although a certain 'human community' doubtless exists outside Christ, and millions of people are searching for it today in the West's depersonalized technocracy, yet we must maintain that 'Christian fellowship' is something different in kind. It has a supernatural origin and quality, for it involves fellowship with God as well as with his people. A Christian congregation which calls people to conversion and so to church membership must exhibit visibly 'the grace of Christ, the love of God and the fellowship of the Holy Spirit.'

CONVERSION AND SOCIETY

Thirdly we must examine the relation between conversion and social responsibility. The report of Bangkok's Section I included the statement that 'personal conversion always leads to social action.' This is so, or should be so. For a convert to Jesus Christ lives in the world as well as in the church, and has responsibilities to the world as well as to the church. I think it is the tendency of churches to 'ecclesiasticize' their members which has made so many modern Christians understandably wary of conversion and church membership. Conversion must not take the convert out of the world but rather send him back into it, the same person in the same world, and yet a new person with new convictions and new standards. If Jesus's first command was 'come!,' his second was 'go!,' that is, we are to go back into the world out of which we have come, and go back as Christ's ambassadors.

The report *The Church for Others* alluded to this tension:

> The biblical view of conversion envisages a double movement, the turning away from preoccupation with one's own interest and the turning towards the interests of the neighbour (Philippians 2:3). It is a movement of turning away from the world in that the terms of the world, based on self-interest, can no longer be accepted. At the same time, it is a turning *towards* the world, now seen from the perspective of hope, in the light of God's purpose.

With his customary simplicity, Lord Ramsey summed up the alternatives in one of his pre-ordination charges entitled 'The Priest and Politics.' He said:

> I suggest that there are three broadly contrasted procedures. It is possible to preach the gospel of conversion without any sight of its social context. It is possible to preach a social gospel which omits the reality of conversion to Christ. Be it your wisdom to preach the gospel of conversion, making it clear that it is the whole man with all his relationships who is converted to Jesus as the Lord of all he is and does.
>
> *The Christian Priest Today*, SPCK, *1972*

Commitment to Christ involves commitment to the world to which and for which he came.

In October 1973 during the course of a mission in the University of Dar-es-Salaam, I was given the privilege of a brief audience of President Julius Nyerere. We talked about the degree of Christians' involvement in Tanzania's national development. Mwalimu (as Tanzanians call their leader with affectionate respect) then said with great emphasis: 'I myself am involved. Every Christian should be involved. I sometimes ask people who call themselves "committed Christians" what they are committed to. Christ was committed to people. We should be also.'

CONVERSION AND CULTURE

Fourthly I come to the question of conversion and human culture. We have already touched on it when discussing church membership. Let me now introduce the subject in this way. Some people think and talk about conversion as if it involved no great upheaval, and little if any change in the convert's life-style. Others seem to expect such a complete change as virtually to fumigate the convert from all the supposed contamination of his former culture. But conversion is not the automatic renunciation of all our inherited culture. True, conversion involves repentance, and repentance is renunciation. Yet this does not require the convert to step right out of his former culture into a Christian sub-culture which is totally distinctive. Sometimes we seem to expect him to withdraw from the real world altogether!

In both West and East it is vital for us to learn to distinguish between Scripture and culture, and between those things in culture which are inherently evil and must therefore be renounced for Christ's sake and those things which are good or indifferent and may therefore be retained, even transformed and enriched. In the West, according to the authors of *God's Lively People* (Fontana, 1971),

. . . our congregations demand from every new member not only a conversion but also a change in culture. He has to abandon some of his contemporary behaviour and to accept the older patterns prevalent among the majority of the congregation. The new Christian has to learn the old hymns and to appreciate them. He has to learn the language of the pulpit. He has to share in some conservative political opinions. He has to dress a bit oldfashioned . . . In brief, he has to step back two generations and undergo what one may call a painful cultural circumcision.

Similarly, Bishop David Sheppard writes that 'few are able to be as objective as the shop steward who said that churches require you to do a crash course in middle class behaviour, rather than to learn Christian maturity' (*Built as a City*).

In the Third World too, and wherever a non-Christian religion dominates a country's culture, Christians need great wisdom to discern between what may be retained and what must be renounced. In many cases new converts adopt too negative an attitude to their former culture. This may have several serious consequences. Christians who break loose entirely from the society in which they were nurtured may find themselves rootless and insecure, and may even—with conventional restraints removed—lapse into moral licence. They may even develop a Christian 'communalism' which gives them a new security in which to live but cuts them off from their former friends and relatives. Also they may arouse opposition. When Christians are seen as undermining the fabric of traditional society, they are regarded as dangerous fanatics and provoke fierce irrational hostility. There have been examples of this from the earliest days of the church, as when the Jews accused Stephen of teaching 'that this Jesus of Nazareth will . . . change the customs which Moses delivered to us' and when some merchants of Philippi accused Paul and Silas of 'disturbing our city' because 'they advocate customs which it is not lawful for us Romans to accept or practise' (Acts 6:14; 16:20, 21). In both cases, although one context was Jewish and the other Roman, the issue concerned 'customs,' either the abandonment of old customs or the introduction of new ones. Culture consists of customs, and people feel threatened when their customs are disturbed. Of course, in one sense Jesus Christ is always a disturber of the peace, because he challenges all inherited custom, convention and tradition, and insists that the whole of life must come under his scrutiny and judgment. Yet it is not a necessary part of our Christian allegiance to be iconoclasts, and to destroy the culture of the past for no better reason than that it is old or that it was part of our pre-conversion life. Culture is ambivalent because man himself is ambivalent. As the Lausanne Covenant expressed it: 'Because man is God's creature, some of his culture is rich in beauty and goodness. Because he has fallen, all of it is tainted with sin and some of it is demonic' (para. 10). So 'culture must always be tested and judged by Scripture,' and we need discernment to evaluate it.

Writing against a Moslem background, Bishop Kenneth Cragg sums up well the relation between conversion and culture:

Baptism, bringing persons within the church, means their incorporation by faith into the supranational fellowship of Christ. It does not, properly understood, deculturalise the new believer; it enchurches him. That 'enchurchment,' as its impact widens, bears creatively upon all areas of its context. The new Christian becomes responsible to Christ for his old setting and to his old setting in the new truth. But he is not thereby 'going foreign.' All that is not incompatible with Christ goes with him into baptism. Conversion is not 'migration'; it is the personal discovery of the meaning of the universal Christ within the old framework of race, language and tradition.

The Call of the Minaret, Lutterworth, 1956

CONVERSION AND THE HOLY SPIRIT

The fifth and last aspect of conversion to be developed is its relation to the work of the Holy Spirit. This is the note on which I believe it is right to conclude, for much of what I have written thus far may have seemed too man-centred and man-confident. Mission, I have urged, is what *we* are sent into the world to do. In evangelism *we* do the proclaiming and in dialogue *we* do the listening. Salvation is what *we* long that our friends will receive. And conversion describes (even in the New Testament) what *we* do, both when we ourselves turn to Christ and when we turn others to Christ. Thus people are said in the Acts to 'turn to the Lord' (*eg* 9:35; 11:21), and Jesus himself spoke of our need to 'turn' and humble ourselves like children if we are ever to enter God's kingdom (Matthew 18:3, 4). Also John the Baptist was to 'turn many of the sons of Israel to the Lord their God' (Luke 1:16), while the apostle Paul was to 'turn' many Gentiles 'from darkness to light and from the power of Satan to God' (Acts 26:17, 18, *cf* v20 and James 5:19, 20). But all this language of human activity is seriously misleading if it is taken to mean that in the end mission is a human work and conversion a human achievement.

This is precisely the impression which we often give, however. In this pragmatic age the church easily slips into the outlook of the world and supposes that the key to evangelistic success is business efficiency. So we publish our manuals of instruction on do-it-yourself evangelism and perfect our ecclesiastical methodologies. Mind you, I happen myself to believe in efficiency, and have never found any reason why Christians should be conspicuous for their inefficiency! At the same time, we must never degrade evangelism into being merely or even mainly a technique to be learned or a formula to be recited. Some people seem to look forward with relish to the time when the evangelistic work of the church will be computerized, the whole job will be done by machines instead of people, and the evangelization of the world will be the ultimate triumph of human technology.

In contrast to the proud self-confident mood of the modern age the apostles' humble reliance on the power of the Holy Spirit stands out in bold relief. They believed (and we should believe with them) that man is dead in trespasses and sins, blind to spiritual truth, and a slave of sin and Satan. In consequence, he cannot 'turn' himself or save himself. Nor can any other man 'turn' him or save him. Only the Holy Spirit can open his eyes, enlighten his darkness, liberate him from bondage, turn him to God and bring him out of death into life. Certainly repentance and faith are plainly declared in the New Testament to be the duty of men (Acts 2:38; 16:31; 17:30), but, as we have seen, they are also the gift of God (*eg* Acts 11:18; Ephesians 2:8; Philippians 1:29). And however perplexing this antinomy may be, it is necessary in our man-centred world to assert it, so that we may humble ourselves before God.

We are all familiar with the development of modern psychological techniques—in advertising (overt and subliminal), in government propaganda, in the deliberate inducement of mass hysteria, and in that most wicked assault on the human personality called 'brain-washing.' But we Christians must make it clear beyond all doubt that evangelism is an entirely different kind of activity (whatever Dr William Sargent may say in his famous

Battle for the Mind, Heinemann, 1957). We must refuse to try to bludgeon people into the kingdom of God. The very attempt is an insult to the dignity of human beings and a sinful usurpation of the prerogatives of the Holy Spirit. It is also unproductive. For one inevitable result of evangelism by unlawful means (what Paul called 'disgraceful, underhanded ways,' 2 Corinthians 4:2) is the leakage from the church of those whose conversion has thus been 'engineered.'

Some words of caution now need to be added, lest we draw unwarranted deductions from the necessity of the Holy Spirit's work in evangelism. Let me mention briefly four conclusions which trust in the Holy Spirit cannot justify. The first is slipshod preparation. 'There is no need for me to prepare before preaching,' somebody argues; 'I shall rely on the Holy Spirit to give me the words. Jesus himself promised that it would be given us in that hour what we are to say.' Such talk sounds plausible, until we remember that the misquotation of Scripture is the devil's game. Jesus was referring to the hour of persecution not of proclamation, and to the prisoner's dock in a law court, not the pulpit in a church. Trust in the Holy Spirit is not intended to save us the bother of preparation. The Holy Spirit can indeed give us utterance if we are suddenly called upon to speak and there has been no opportunity to prepare. But he can also clarify and direct our thinking in our study. Indeed, experience suggests that he does a better job there than in the pulpit.

Next, trust in the Holy Spirit cannot justify a general anti-intellectualism. The 'lofty words and wisdom' which Paul renounced were not doctrinal preaching or the use of his mind, but the popular wisdom of the world and the fancy rhetoric of the Greeks. In contrast to the former he determined to be loyal to the foolish message of the cross, and in contrast to the latter he would rely in his human weakness on 'the demonstration of the Spirit and of power' (1 Corinthians 2:1–5). But Paul was no anti-intellectual. His sermons were full of doctrinal substance and reasoning. He and his fellow-apostles were not just heralds announcing good news; they were advocates arguing a case. As Wolfhart Pannenberg has written:

An otherwise unconvincing message cannot attain the power to convince simply by appealing to the Holy Spirit . . . The convincingness of the Christian message can stem only from its contents. Where this is not the case, the appeal to the Holy Spirit is no help at all to the preacher . . . Argumentation and the operation of the Holy Spirit are not in competition with each other. In trusting in the Spirit Paul in no way spared himself thinking or arguing.

Basic Questions in Theology, Vol. II, SCM, 1971

Thirdly, trust in the Holy Spirit cannot be used to justify irrelevance. Some say rather piously that the Holy Spirit is himself the complete and satisfactory solution to the problem of communication, and indeed that when he is present and active, then communication ceases to be a problem. What on earth does such a statement mean? Do we now have liberty to be as obscure, confused and irrelevant as we like, and the Holy Spirit will make all things plain? To use the Holy Spirit to rationalize our laziness is nearer blasphemy than piety. Of course *without* the Holy Spirit all our explanations are futile. But this is not to say that *with* the Holy Spirit they are also futile. For the Holy Spirit chooses to work through them. Trust in the Holy Spirit must not be used as a device to save us the labour of biblical and contemporary studies.

Fourthly, trust in the Holy Spirit does not justify the suppression of our personality. Some seem to imagine that if the Holy Spirit is to be in full control, they must entirely eliminate themselves. But what doctrine of the Spirit is this? Our understanding of biblical inspiration should have protected us from this mistake. For in the process we call 'inspiration,' the Spirit did not suppress the personality of the human authors, but first fashioned and then fully used it. Although modern Christian communicators cannot lay claim to a comparable inspiration, they may be sure that the same Spirit has no wish to obliterate their personality either.

What is forbidden us is all rhetorical affection, all deliberate contriving of effect, all artificiality, hypocrisy and play acting, all standing in front of the mirror in order self-consciously to plan our gestures and grimaces, all self-advertisement and self-reliance. More positively we are to be ourselves, to be natural, to develop and exercise the gifts which God has given us, and at the same time to rest our confidence not in ourselves but in the Holy Spirit who deigns to work through us.

All down its history, the Christian church seems to have oscillated from one extreme to the other. At times it is so wordly that it goes to the extreme of self-confidence, as if evangelism were merely a question of business efficiency and human technique. At other times it becomes so other-wordly that it goes to the opposite extreme of self-depreciation, as if evangelism were entirely the work of the Holy Spirit and we had nothing whatever to contribute. But a truly biblical understanding of the purpose of the Spirit to work through some men to lead others to conversion would deliver us from both these extremes of self-reliance and self-despair, of pride and laziness.

What Scripture lays upon us instead is the need for a proper combination of humility and humanity—the humility to let God be God, acknowledging that he alone can give sight to the blind and life to the dead, and the humanity to be ourselves as he has made us, not suppressing our personal individuality, but exercising our God-given gifts and offering ourselves to God as instruments of righteousness in his hand. I wonder if anything is more needed for the Christian mission in the modern age than this healthy fusion of humility and humanity in our reliance on the power of the Holy Spirit.